Wearing God's Mala
THE SEVA SUTRAS

Wearing God's Mala
THE SEVA SUTRAS

SWAMI KHECARANATHA

Other books by Swami Khecaranatha

Depth Over Time: Kundalini Sadhana,
A Path of Transformation and Liberation (2010)

Merging With the Divine: One Day at a Time (2011)

The Heart of Recognition: The Wisdom and Practices
of the Pratyabhijna Hrdayam (2013)

Shiva's Trident: The Consciousness of Freedom
and the Means to Liberation (2013).

More information about his practice, books, and meditation CDs is available at *SwamiKhecaranatha.com.*

This book is dedicated to Śiva,
the servant of servants.

In appreciation,

Swami Khecaranatha

ACKNOWLEDGMENTS

This book is the result of the work of a team of people whose many talents have brought it to published form. I am grateful for their assistance and wish to extend my thanks to all of them.

I want to express my gratitude to my editor, Ellen Jefferds, for her dedication and professionalism in editing the book, and for her meticulous work in creating the layout of the interior.

I am grateful to Christine Sheridan, Sassi LaMuth, and Sonia Foscoli, who read early drafts of the manuscript and provided feedback that helped to improve the book. Christine also performed the invaluable work of copyediting the final version.

Thanks to Keith Jefferds for his assistance with the cover design.

Thank you to my friend Lubosh Cech for the photo of the Śiva lingam on the front cover, and to Scott Eaton for the photos used on the back cover.

Next, I want to acknowledge the artist Ekabhūmi Charles Ellik, who created the exquisite renderings of Śiva and Parā.

Above all, I wish to express my gratitude to my gurus, Bhagavan Nityananda and Swami Rudrananda, at whose feet I gratefully serve.

NOTE ABOUT SANSKRIT TERMS

Throughout this book diacritics are used when spelling any Sanskrit words that have not been assimilated into English. To aid readers unfamiliar with diacritics, the English equivalents are provided the first time important words appear that have significantly different spelling. In addition, readers may wish to refer to the Pronunciation Guide in Appendix A, located on page 301.

Please note, however, that the fonts chosen for the book title, headers, sutras, and callouts do not provide an option for diacritical marks. In such cases, English spellings are given.

INTRODUCTION:

knowing and serving god

You're gonna have to serve somebody, yes indeed,
You're gonna have to serve somebody.
Well, it may be the devil or it may be the Lord,
but you're gonna have to serve somebody.

These lyrics by Bob Dylan succinctly express the importance of serving. I feel very blessed to have learned the value of seva at a young age. When I met my teacher, Swami Rudrananda (Rudi), in 1971 I was immediately filled with gratitude for the opportunity to change my life by opening to higher consciousness. The only response to that gratitude was service. I have served my teacher by doing my inner work and accepting the responsibility he conferred on me of being a lineage carrier in his tradition. My own practice has been grounded in, cultivated in, and allowed to bloom within the sacred temple of service—service to God, to the freedom within myself, to my teachers, and to those around me.

A JOURNEY OF COMMITMENT

Throughout the past forty-plus years, my willingness to come back to my commitment to serve has been the fire of my *sādhana*

(spiritual practice). In all of the hard work, decades of meditation, and the service and engagement in the world, my commitment anchored me. It has been the laser focus that kept me directed whenever it wasn't easy, when I didn't want to serve. Commitment is what enabled me to go on when my resistance surfaced and my mind was complaining, "I shouldn't have to do this . . . why should I have to when they don't have to?" and that whole comic book discussion that goes on in our thoughts.

I have worked very hard, but my experience has been that it was never difficult to hold on to what I knew I wanted in life. The challenge and the difficulty is in living that commitment. Making a commitment is the easy part. Once we affirm, "This is what I'll do," all of our resistance and tension come up. That's when our wish to grow is really tested, and commitment is what must tether us to our practice. Otherwise, what value is our decision to serve if we only live up to it when it's easy?

The really good news about spiritual commitment is that when we first make it, we usually have no clue about the depth of work that will be required to hold on to that commitment. Perhaps being ignorant is part of God's grace! We start down the path of commitment to service, and take one step after the other. We must each discover the work within ourselves, but I will never suggest that you do anything I haven't done myself. You choose whether that's your life. I'm just presenting the options— but I can say without hesitation that whatever level of mastery I have achieved in my spiritual practice has been based on the foundation of seva. All of it.

EVERYTHING IS CONSCIOUSNESS

Let's now look at the overall context and scope of spiritual practice. We can start with a simple statement: Everything is Consciousness. It is the source of all life as well as the *power* of life itself. The purpose of spiritual practice is to understand and directly experience this ultimate truth, and furthermore, to discover that we *are* that Consciousness. In the Kashmir Shaivite tradition of Anuttara Trika, this all-pervading Consciousness is called Śiva (Shiva). He exists in a state of eternal completeness, simply repeating, *Aham,* "I am." That mantra expresses His divine status and it also gives life to us. *Aham* is the very breath of Śiva.

Kashmir Shaivism describes five essential powers of Śiva. The first is that of Consciousness itself. Then, emerging from within Śiva's infinite Consciousness is Śakti (Shakti), the divine energy that creates, sustains, and dissolves the universe, again and again. Tantric exposition clearly states that this power is inherent in the very nature of Consciousness itself. It is not just inert. Śakti is the power of bliss, and arising from bliss are the triadic powers of will, knowledge, and action.

shiva's dynamic powers are the expression of his joy and his intent to expand his freedom through manifestation

Consciousness, bliss, will, knowledge, and action are the source of everything that exists, including our own individuated life. All of creation manifests as an expression of Śiva's unity, arising from within Himself through His five powers for the purpose of expanding His joy and freedom. From within Śiva come all the energies that sustain and illuminate our experience and provide the means to discover our unity with our source.

We learn to access our own divinity by aligning ourselves with these powers. Śiva gives us the capacity to know unconditional joy by knowing Him as our Self. From the highest perspective, this means that Śiva can look back at Himself through us. Consciousness has two essential aspects. One is *prakāśa* (prakasha) the light that illuminates life, and the other is *vimarśa* (vimarsha), the power of Consciousness to know itself. It is through this self-reflective capacity that we, as individuated expressions of the Divine, can know ourselves to be Śiva. We find this knowledge in the simplicity of living in the perfection of our own existence. We don't have to do anything else. In fact, everything else often obscures that realization, because we misunderstand the nature of our life and our relationship to God.

Śiva's divine powers of will, knowledge, and action are traditionally referred to as goddesses. Parā is the supreme goddess of Śiva's will, the ultimate power of His intention to create. This power of will arises from bliss for the sole purpose of expanding Śiva's own state of perfection, joy, and freedom. Knowing this to be the purpose of creation, Śiva then, through the power of action, unfolds all of life. Tantric tradition therefore delineates that there are three aspects of the supreme goddess— Parā (will), Parāparā (knowledge), and Aparā (action). They are all part of the one goddess who embodies the triadic energy of *kuṇḍalini*.

However, when we talk about the three goddesses or powers, we can never separate them. They are like a three-legged table. All three legs must be there or it's going to fall over. The three goddesses simply reflect the different ways that Śiva's light shines forth. God's powers are also the means by which we engage and experience life. We all have a wish, we all have a will, and we do something with it, we all seek to know ourselves, and we act a lot. All of that is the expression of those supreme powers in us.

This understanding about higher consciousness and our relationship with God's powers is not theory. It has been the direct experience of many great saints, teachers, and spiritual practitioners. But if it is to have real meaning, it must become *our* experience—not just during the time we spend meditating, but in every moment of our lives. Otherwise, any discussion of spirituality is just words on a page, based on someone else's realization. It is our commitment to actualizing this highest potential for ourselves that is the bedrock of spiritual practice.

A JOURNEY OF SELF-DISCOVERY

In this book we'll explore in depth how Śiva's powers not only created us, but are the powers we function from as individuals. Furthermore, we'll see that spiritual practice is the transformation of our experience and understanding of those powers as we move beyond our individual perspective. I have written twenty-one sutras to help you discover, within yourself, that you are Śiva. You are universal Consciousness made manifest by the powers of Parā, Parāparā, and Aparā. Śiva's powers are active as *parā kuṇḍalinī*, creating, sustaining, and living as us. And, as some traditions would say, God made us in His own image. *Sādhana* is for us to discover that, in the vibrant reality of our own awareness.

shiva's powers are active as para kundalini, creating, sustaining, and living as us

There are many ways we can understand the progression of our experience from one of duality to being immersed in unity. These sutras will view that transformation through the lens of seva. Sutras are aphorisms—simple, short revelations of truth. They are written as comprehensive teachings on a particular topic, and each is intended to be complete in itself. Like the facets of a prism, every sutra offers a slightly different vantage point from which to understand the progression of the teachings. As we explore the various aspects of *sādhana* in the light of service, we come to recognize that it is through our wish to experience the highest awareness—by using our conscious choice to serve our own source, to serve God—that we can penetrate through every misunderstanding we have.

WHAT IT MEANS TO WEAR GOD'S MALA

I have entitled this book *Wearing God's Māla* because when you receive a *māla*, you are receiving and accepting a commitment. Typically you receive a *māla* from a teacher, so you're receiving their commitment to you. And you're accepting your own commitment not only to that teacher but to your own freedom. By putting on God's *māla*, you are making a commitment to serve the highest in yourself, to expand your willingness and capacity to serve God. So should you choose to take on that practice, understand what you're committing yourself to.

To make this *sādhana* more experiential, I'll be giving four mantras, accompanied by guided meditations. Mantras are resonance, and as we work with them, they function like a radio dial, tuning us in to that particular frequency. The *Mahā Mantra* is: "I offer myself into Your service, without thought of price. Do with me as You wish." This is Śiva's mantra. He says to us, in every moment, "I offer Myself into your service, without thought of price. Do with Me as you wish." How do we respond to such unconditionality? Why not say, "I offer myself back to You"? That would be the highest expression of our own consciousness and bliss.

Selfless service is the unconditional offering of our life to God, and we do that by accessing and expressing the supreme powers of will, knowledge, and action. The next three mantras help actualize that initial offering: "May my will be Your will," "May I know You as my Self," and, "May all my actions serve You." Using these mantras and internalizing their resonances aligns our individual will, knowledge, and action with Śiva's infinite powers. In addition, to establish a more palpable contact with that higher resonance, during the guided meditations we will learn to bring our awareness to *dvādaśānta*—the space about twelve inches above the head—the abode of Parā, Parāparā, and Aparā. At the end of the book I will present a 108-day practice of using these mantras and meditations to deepen your connection with God's power. This is how we pierce the veils of duality, the experience we have that "I am separate, I am different, and I am the doer."

only when we learn to serve unconditionally, without injecting our own needs and desires into the equation, is our desire to serve actualized

The entire practice, the discussion of the sutras, and the mantras and meditations are all given to help you make contact with Śiva's Consciousness and to align you with His powers. Through this inner realization, we learn that we *are* Śiva, and that His powers are our own. But we must then express this realization in life—and therefore much of our discussion will focus on how we engage the world from clarity and depth. Although we're ultimately serving God, we appear to be serving those around us, and navigating the practical aspects of service is part of the challenge. Only when we learn to serve unconditionally, without injecting our own needs and desires into the equation, is our desire to serve actualized. Only then can we say that we embody the spirit of the *mala* we wear.

the seva sutras

sutra one

these teachings are meant for those who wish to awaken, for
those who, full of worship and reverence, wish to experience and
express their highest consciousness through selfless service to god.

sutra two

autonomous, absolute consciousness always exists—it is the
light that illuminates all of life. the divine self is not a reality
previously unknown because it knows itself. paramashiva
looks back at himself through each of his five faces.

sutra three

emerging from the bliss of that self-reflective aspect of
consciousness (the light by which all of life is seen), are the
triadic powers of will, knowledge, and action. these are the
energies of creation—from the manifest universe to the individual.

sutra four

divine light travels through the heart of consciousness as the
emission of those powers to express itself as the individual, and
then rises back to itself as the light of the sushumna.

sutra five

hold fast to the lamp of sadhana and your own light
will merge with the universal light shining forth
to illuminate the perfection of your life.

sutra six

shiva's supreme powers are the same powers by which
the individual serves him. service is the charnel grounds,
ablaze with the fire of consciousness, that burns
away all limited capacity to give.

sutra seven

the sadhaka learns to serve those divine powers by
following the master's teachings, contemplating the
wisdom of revealed scripture, and through direct experience.
in that service he receives the fullness of shiva's grace and
achieves jivanmukti, authentic liberation in this lifetime.

sutra eight

liberation is the dissolving of the veils of duality
that shroud and limit the experience of pure awareness.

sutra nine

the light of consciousness that illuminates the darkness
and illusion of dualistic experience shines forth through
union with the goddess para. she is the one who serves
as the power of shiva's divine will.

sutra ten

the upayas—the means to liberation—are an
ascending capacity to serve the goddess shakti.

sutra eleven

shiva is known and served through para's action,
grounded in knowledge. the result of all action should
be the discovery of the knowledge of the self.

sutra twelve

the authentic devotee of shiva sacrifices everything
in service to him. this unconditional service requires
the surrendering of self-serving identity.

sutra thirteen

freedom from attachment, which is the primary binding
agent of limited identity, is attained through stilling
the fluctuations of the mind.

sutra fourteen

the perpetual search for something outside of ourselves
in order to be happy is the source of unhappiness.
the actions of that incessant reaching contract the
highest will into limited desire. from that limited need we
act to serve ourselves, creating the wheel of karma.

sutra fifteen

to be free of the endless traversing across the
ocean of incarnation you must see the face of god
everywhere you look.

sutra sixteen

we worship god so that we may know supreme
consciousness as it knows itself.

sutra seventeen

surrendering everything to god is made possible
when one attains identity with him through meditation
and selfless service.

sutra eighteen

surrendering all activities to shiva, the sadhaka is freed
from the veil of misunderstanding that he is the doer.

sutra nineteen

stillness is the highest form of worship and service to god.

sutra twenty

surrender is the key. it is in surrender that we experience
the stillness of consciousness in the center of the divine heart.

sutra twenty-one

it is in stillness that we merge into presence—the divine light
from which we came. we have served god's purpose.

the mantras of service

i offer myself into your service,
without thought of price—
do with me as you wish

may my will be your will

may i know you as myself

may all my actions serve you

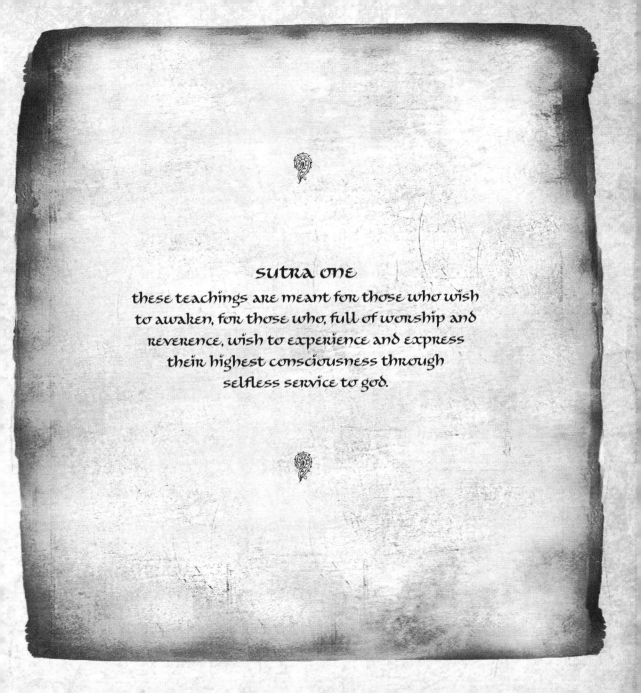

SUTRA ONE

these teachings are meant for those who wish
to awaken, for those who, full of worship and
reverence, wish to experience and express
their highest consciousness through
selfless service to god.

Sutras are concise expressions that encapsulate spiritual teachings. Traditionally, they always start with the highest knowledge, and then more detailed explanations unfold. In that sense, there would be no reason to elaborate further if one could simply grasp the full significance of the highest teaching, so let's start by discussing what is meant in this first sutra.

Grace is a gift from God. We have been given the opportunity to know and love the Divine—to experience a lifetime of growth and celebration. Grace is the innate understanding that's awakened within us that we are none other than the Consciousness from which everything is created. When we receive the gift of grace, how could we respond in any way except to offer ourselves in gratitude and serve the giver? This is the wellspring of seva, of true selfless service. Grace appears in many forms, but it is essentially the activation of a higher awareness within us that can rise out of the density of our limited experience back to itself, back to the experience of unity. Once that activation happens, we must respond to grace in order for it to fully flower in us.

You may or may not have had some gigantic, rapturous "I am everything" experience. Perhaps there was just a taste of something beyond your own limited awareness. Even reading a book such as this is an expression of some impulse within you seeking to grow spiritually. Whatever your experience to date, what you have to understand is that liberation is available to you and that ultimately, only one thing frees us, and that is Śiva's grace. Once that grace begins to stir within us, it will rise and reveal its source. This is how we come to experience that God is none other than our Self—the pure subject who perceives, enjoys, reflects, thinks, and senses—as well as being the agent of Consciousness in whom all possible forms of experience reside.

THE ROLE OF SEVA

Seva is centered in a profoundly simple place within. The desire to serve arises from the merging of our heart with the heart of God, in a state of complete surrender. We receive grace in the depth of our heart, and it is out of that depth that we express our gratitude in the form of service. Selfless service is simply the natural expression of the love, gratitude, and devotion we feel. We may sometimes remember the resonance of grace; we wake up and spontaneously feel grateful. Other days, we may feel like an inert lump, and feel the pain of knowing that we're definitely not yet Śiva! Then, our effort is to find some openness, to find our heart. What we must not do is acquiesce and say, "Oh, I don't feel my heart. What I feel is all this tension, or all this suffering, so I'll express that."

Students sometimes tell me that they don't meditate because their mind is too busy. What kind of reasoning is that? The purpose of meditation is to find the inner place that does make contact with a different dimension of awareness. We make that connection again and again and again, so that we learn the path home. Then, through seva, we extend ourselves and express that experience in our lives. This is the highest seva. We are serving Śiva, who simply wants to live as us, instead of us and all our stuff. Instead of wallowing in our misery—I feel sad, I'm pissed off, I'm this, I'm that, I'm longing—and functioning from this level of limitation, we must reach deeper in ourselves and say, "No! I will function from openness and joy." This gives us a hint that seva is not necessarily an action—although it often is expressed as such—but an awareness, a state of consciousness.

Seva is defined as selfless service because we are not serving ourselves. Furthermore, we are not serving only when we want to or just those we think we want to serve. We're trying to develop the capacity to access supreme Consciousness, and the five powers inherent within it. So we choose to practice seva for the purpose of freeing ourselves of our inability to tune in to that awareness and those powers, and to maintain that connection no matter what arises in life. To accomplish that we will have to let go of our own limited perspective.

For many years I served the ashram I lived in by working in a bakery. It was a business that employed many people in our community, so it was very significant in that sense, but there were many times during those years that I did not want to be doing that job. I encountered tremendous resistance within myself. I was the head teacher in the ashram under the swami and initially

seva is defined as selfless service because we are not serving ourselves

I felt I was too important to work in the bakery fifteen hours a day. It was seven days a week of literally getting up at four in the morning in order to get started at four-thirty. We worked until a quarter to six in the evening, ran home (most of the time not having showered), went to meditation class, and then back to the bakery—often until nine at night.

That was not fun, and I generally did not experience extreme joy at the thought of heading out each morning. Yet it was amazing, because every day, in the middle of my resistance and grumbling, I had to remember why I was there. I recognized that the effort required of me in this job played a critical component in developing the ability to surrender my own needs. I learned that in serving the ashram, I was really serving the God within me—because I had to break down all my resistance, remain open, and find Him, no matter what I was doing.

if living in god and serving his will is not the most important thing in your life, you will not have it and you will not do it

WHAT IS THE MOST IMPORTANT THING IN YOUR LIFE?

I'm going to make this unequivocal statement: If living in God and serving His will is not the most important thing in your life, you will not have it and you will not do it. Something else will become more important. What's truly amazing is that it's not our families, our lovers, or our bank accounts that we make more important, but our own tension. Have all the lovers you want, have all the money you want, have everything. It's not relevant. My teacher Rudi said it clearly: "The only thing you have to surrender is your tension."

The key element of that tension is the deep-seated suffering caused by our separation from God. This primal pain expresses itself as all the things that cause us to shut down and get tense. It manifests as all the trivialities we believe are the cause of our tension: somebody looked at me wrong, or they didn't look at me right, etcetera. We narrow our life into those superficial levels of tension and we make that the most important thing in our lives. And as we all know, we feed the things that are important to us. What if you made opening your heart the highest priority?

Every moment, in every experience we have, we choose what is most important to us. Even when we feel our resistance, we can either get caught in it or we can learn and open from it. It doesn't really matter what form resistance takes; the specific idea or emotion we get stuck in is irrelevant. The conscious person recognizes that this level of disturbance is like the aftershocks of an earthquake. The real shaking happens in the core of the earth, releasing the deep tension, pressure, and resistance located there. When that earthquake happens in you, don't believe your mind or your emotions. Just be grateful that some tension is being kicked loose. When you find yourself nitpicking on the surface of life, realize that you're functioning in that kind of reverberation, get your seismic meter out, and start looking for the source of that release. Don't just function on the level of the aftershocks.

Unfortunately, we often choose to hold on to the very surface tensions that we need to surrender. We therefore need to pay attention to what we're not letting go of. What part of your body, your mind, your emotions, your experience in life are you holding on to? We have to be grateful when we discover our limitations, even when we feel a rock in our heart, because we need to let go on all levels. Most people never feel anything but "I am a rock," and they continually sing that song. They think they're separate, and they work hard to perpetuate that state. We create our own experience, and if we extend and function from a place of separation, then the life we have designed, cultivated, and carefully tweaked is an expression of that separation.

Given this tendency to perpetuate our limited perspective, service is vitally important in that it breaks down our self-imposed restrictions. Look at the life of the sage Milarepa. His teacher said, "Build me a house." Milarepa built a house, and his teacher said, "You idiot, I didn't want a stone house. I wanted a wooden house." So Milarepa built a wooden house. "You double idiot. I didn't want a wooden house here, I wanted a wooden house over there." This went on for fourteen years. It's a true story. Milarepa's teacher was breaking down every level of resistance and perspective in him. Modern-day students should be so lucky!

WHO DO YOU SERVE?

what are you willing to change in order to selflessly serve god?

Who do you really serve? Think about that honestly—and don't be surprised when you come to the conclusion that you're serving yourself. So here's the next question: What are you willing to change? Not, what are other people required to do to change, or, I'll do it if other people do it. What are *you* willing to change in order to selflessly serve God? The key element to consider is this: <u>Will you allow yourself to *be changed*? What</u> we're willing to change is very different from whether we allow ourselves to be changed. Usually we're only willing to change if it doesn't cost anything, but it's easy to give away an old shirt you never liked.

These are the questions you have to ask yourself if you truly want to selflessly serve God. Is unfolding the capacity to serve the most important thing in your life? Because as soon as we say, "Yes," we start to recognize who we really serve. And we begin to understand what changes are required within us in order to live up to that commitment. <u>We surrender ourselves unconditionally</u> by stating, "<u>I will serve You with my life. I offer myself into Your service, without thought of price. Do with me as You wish." Do you have the courage to do that?</u>

It's a blessing that even when we say, "Yes, I do," we must affirm that despite the fact that we don't yet understand what it means to make such a statement. This is part of grace. When I felt I'd made an unconditional commitment to serve my teacher, his plane crashed into a mountain and I had to come to grips with that loss. Was I going to let that event devastate me for ten thousand years, or could I rise above my own need and celebrate Rudi's freedom? For the first thirty seconds I wasn't sure which it was going to be. Only grace said, "Wake up! What's happening here? What are you paying attention to? Your own suffering, or your teacher's liberation?"

<u>We must experience our own resistance before we can free</u> ourselves from it. Rudi said it clearly: "If you're not feeling your

is unfolding the capacity to serve the most important thing in your life?

resistance, you're not working." Grace, as it awakens, will push out everything that's in the way of expressing its own joy. It will push out all limitation on the levels of the body, senses, mind, and emotion—and it will all be burned in the fire of Consciousness. Our practice is to consciously offer ourselves into that fire. Only grace frees, but we can choose to ignore that openness and go back to the confines of whatever it was that we were doing. We must choose a higher experience in every moment.

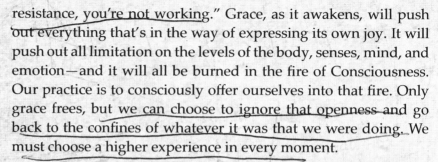

We cannot allow the conditions in our life to interfere with our decision to open to grace and serve that power. We all experience the pressures of our responsibilities and our interactions with others, but none of that has to affect us. We may think we do not have the capacity to engage the world and be open at the same time, but that thought is itself a limitation that we must let go of. When we live in the confines of our own thought-constructs we don't see the unlimited capacity of God. Nothing restricts Śiva. He can experience the unbounded joy of His own existence and maintain the entire cosmos at the same time! That should give us a hint that we might be able to attend to our daily lives without losing the ability open our hearts and serve.

Living in God and serving Him is not primarily an action, although it will often be expressed on that level. Serving God is a state of being, and from there one can engage in anything. We first have to establish ourselves in that state, and from there, we serve. Too often, we launch ourselves into our day without opening our heart, and then all we do is fight because we started by extending ourselves out. When we take the time to meditate and make contact with our center, and then extend into life, there's no conflict between our inner state and anything we do.

THE POWER OF PRESENCE

We awaken to our own infinite potential through grace, and it often comes in the form of a relationship with a teacher or guru. *Guru* means "dispeller of darkness," not "bringer of light." The light is already there. Grace is simply dispelling the darkness that obscures the light. It's amazing that infinite light can be obscured by darkness, that there's anything bigger than that brilliant illumination. Actually, we should say there's something infinitely smaller than infinite light, and yet it has the power to obscure. That's why we must cultivate Presence and stillness, but even more so, we must look for openness. It has a different *rasa*, a different flavor—one that has the capacity to become bigger than the thing that's making us small.

we cannot allow the conditions in our life to interfere with our decision to open to grace and to serve that power

By tuning in to openness, we find the power of Presence. This is the expansion of energy that is able to absorb, transform, and dissolve any amount of density. It's a dynamic force that transmutes darkness into light, and as it does so, it opens us further. Śiva is not inert. He's dynamic. That's why we talk about His five powers. Consciousness has energy, Śakti, and therefore has the capacity to reveal the highest in us to ourselves. When we focus on aligning our powers with Śiva's by serving Him, we function from His openness. We are able to absorb the darkness, rise above our tension, and dissolve the obscurity.

We can choose to experience the unity in life or continue to suffer in the self-imposed prison of duality. *Svātantrya*, which means "absolute, autonomous freedom," is always ever-present. It is the essence of Consciousness and the fundamental quality of the supreme subject. *Svātantrya* is the nature of the heart of God, and it is the grace of God. Our choice is to discover and live from that level of awareness in ourselves. Then, we bow down in reverence to that grace.

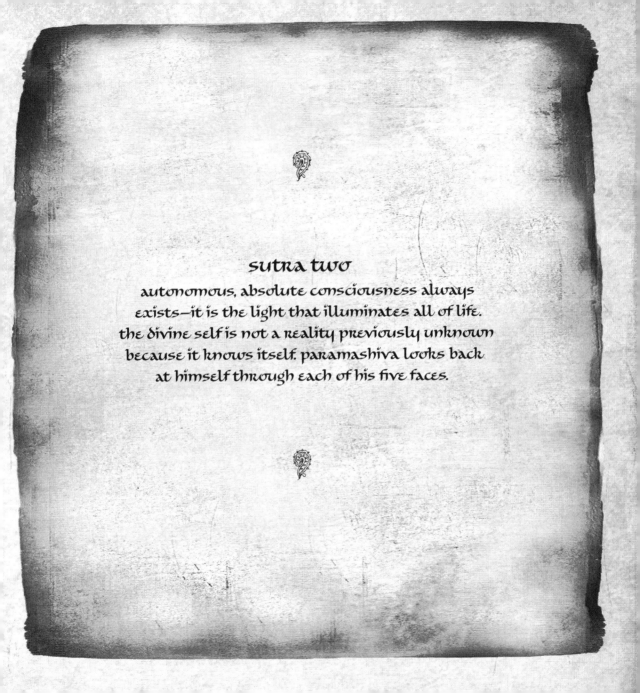

sutra two

autonomous, absolute consciousness always
exists—it is the light that illuminates all of life.
the divine self is not a reality previously unknown
because it knows itself. paramashiva looks back
at himself through each of his five faces.

All reality, both inner and outer, is held within undifferentiated Consciousness in a state of absolute potential. That Consciousness bursts forth as *prakāśa*, the light that illuminates life. Brilliant in its own radiance, this power is an effulgence that continually shines forth from within itself to create all manifestation. The illuminating power of *prakāśa* is present in every level of creation, experienced as infinite light in our own awareness. Although it appears as diversity, *prakāśa* is really the expression of unity, much as light coming through a lattice is broken into parts.

The other essential aspect of Consciousness is *vimarśa*, the ability of Consciousness to be self-aware. Like a mirror, *vimarśa* is the self-reflective capacity of infinite Consciousness to see the light and to recognize itself as the light. It does not depend on anything outside of itself to know itself. Both *prakāśa* and *vimarśa* are inherent in God's nature, and are another way of understanding Śiva and Śakti, the cosmic forces of Consciousness and energy. These two are never separate because underlying the entire universe is a conscious energy. *Prakāśa* and *vimarśa* are the all-embracing fullness of supreme Consciousness.

When Jesus said, "I am the light," He didn't need to add, "I know I'm the light" because it was self-evident to Him. We, on the other hand, have to remind ourselves that this is what we are. This is what *sādhana* is all about. Accessing the power of that self-reflective capacity is the essence of spiritual freedom. It's *vimarśa* that allows us to know our own state, to recognize, "I am Śiva." And because we have Śiva's power of will, we have the ability to change our state if we find that we're not experiencing the highest awareness. We also have the choice not to change, and although God can try to change us, our consciousness won't be transformed if we dig in our heels and refuse His grace.

accessing the power of that self-reflective capacity is the essence of spiritual freedom. it's vimarsha that allows us to know our own state, to recognize, "i am shiva"

OUR SELF-REFLECTIVE CAPACITY

The *tattvas* are a way of mapping out unity and duality, both of which exist within a singular state of oneness. They describe the condensation of consciousness from supreme, infinite pure Consciousness down to inert matter, clearly showing us that Consciousness is inherent in everything. If that is true, however, why are some things less conscious than others? It is due to the diminishing self-reflective capacity to know that one is Consciousness. That is the essence of the descent of Consciousness detailed in the levels of the *tattvas*. A rock does not know that it is actually a condensation of Consciousness. This is the crux of the difference between sentience and insentience. Sentience is the self-reflective capacity to know oneself. This is important to those of us who no longer want to be rocks!

Understand how powerful this is. It is not enough to be conscious. Consciousness must know that it's conscious. It is this self-awareness that creates the dynamism and effulgence that emerge from stillness. The highest state is one of "dynamic stillness" because it is the active expression of bliss, the unconditional joy of knowing who we are. Sutra One established our intention to offer ourselves in order to realize our highest Self. To make that a reality, we have to do the work of dissolving every part of us that does not know and does not believe that we are Śiva. As we do that, the darkness of not knowing will get illuminated, to show us exactly what we need to change.

The very purpose of our life is to know who we are, and Śiva has given us the capacity to discover that within ourselves. We all have the ability to change our own state, to grow beyond whatever level of awareness we function in. When we uncover our limitations, we should only feel grateful that we do recognize that this is the level of awareness we live, function, express, and project from—and we can say, "No. This is not the life that I want." Then we commit to doing the work of changing our consciousness and our behavior.

This commitment is the divine thread that we follow back to its source, where it emerges out of infinite nothingness. It's like a lifeline you can reach for when you're out in the middle of the ocean and the waves are turbulent—when people aren't treating you the way you want, or they're even trying to run over you with their motorboats, and the water's deeper than you thought it was going to be. Even in moments like that, we find our self-awareness and begin to pull ourselves back, out of that disturbance.

If we were not that awareness, and if we didn't have that self-knowledge, we wouldn't have the lifeline. Perhaps that's the essence of purgatory; we'd just be lost, with no way out and no way deeper in. It is because we are an individuated expression of God that we can know our divine status, and we can follow our individuality back to its source. How wonderful is that?

THE FIVE FACES OF GOD

As divine light shines back on itself, it reveals the face of God, which is none other than our own reflection. We can also speak of God as having five faces, which are His five powers of Consciousness, bliss, will, knowledge, and action. Our capacity to see God comes from the ability to know ourselves, to penetrate back through the expression of His powers to their source. And, like God, we do not depend on anything outside of ourselves to know who we are. We have direct access to this highest knowledge, because it is contained within us. To understand this further, let's look at the five faces, the five powers of Śiva, in more detail. These powers correspond to the first five *tattvas*, or levels of Consciousness. If you are unfamiliar with the structure of the *tattvas*, please refer to Appendix C, page 304, where you will find a complete chart of the thirty-seven levels, as well as a brief description of their significance.

The highest *tattva*, *cit śakti* (chit shakti), is the power of Consciousness itself. This is Śiva: infinite, omnipresent Consciousness, which is transcendental, unmanifest, and

the very purpose of our life is to know who we are, and shiva has given us the capacity to discover that within ourselves. we all have the ability to change our own state, to grow beyond whatever level of awareness we function in formless, yet exists within and *as* everything that is created. *Cit śakti* is the source of all other powers, all other energies, and ultimately all manifestation. We've said that Consciousness is a dynamic stillness. It is not an inert Presence because inherent within it is the power to be aware. The reason it's called *cit śakti* is because *śakti* means energy. This is the energy of Consciousness itself, ever-present within our individuated consciousness.

The next level is *ānanda śakti*, the energy of bliss. The first thing that arises out of the power and awareness of Consciousness— before anything else manifests—is the bliss of its own Self, the bliss of its own awareness. The effulgence of this Consciousness is so powerful that it expresses pure, unbounded, unconditional joy from the experience of its own fullness. How amazing to understand that as energy explodes out of Consciousness, it explodes as joy and from joy. This offers us valuable clue about where we wish to point our attention as we work to penetrate through the manifest expression of life back to its source.

The next three *tattvas* are Śiva's powers of will, knowledge, and action. Will, or *icchā śakti*, lives as the goddess Parā. From within Śiva's experience of His own freedom and joy comes the will to perpetually expand that state. If divine will is the expansion of freedom, perfect in its understanding and in its own bliss, then everything that emerges and manifests from it must also be perfect. Śiva knows Himself and exactly what He wants to create in order to share His freedom and express His joy. That power of knowing is *jñāna śakti*, the goddess Parāparā, and the highest knowledge is to know your Self, even if you're Śiva.

From divine will and knowledge, the power to act emerges. Śiva knows what He wants to create in order to share His freedom, and He does that through the power of infinite action, *kriyā śakti*, the goddess Aparā. Śiva's capacity to assume or manifest Himself in any form is a quality of His own nature and is the result of His absolute freedom. Divine action is not directed toward any specific result but is the expression of His own energies, His own Consciousness, and His own bliss.

Held within Śiva's five powers is the potential for all manifestation, but as yet, no form has arisen. Everything that might arise is still in a state of perfect unity, a pure expression of Śiva's experience of joy within His own awareness, without any need for it to be expressed as specific form. This is the experience we seek to have. It is the only experience that liberates us from the perception of duality.

if divine will is the perpetual expansion of freedom, perfect in its understanding and in its own bliss, then everything that emerges and manifests from it must also be perfect

THE POWER OF REVELATION

In Kashmir Shaivism, form is always understood as the *appearance* of duality, not the reality of duality. As human beings our experience in life is in the world of form, and we get so caught up in it that we don't see its source. That's why we have to change where we are focused. It's why we have to penetrate back through the appearance of duality to uncover the unity that underlies all diversity. We never deny the experience of duality, but we must understand that it is a limited experience—that, in fact, there is ultimately no duality, but simply the experience of it.

Traditional texts talk about the fivefold acts of Śiva: creation, maintenance, dissolution, concealment, and revelation. Śiva is constantly creating, maintaining, and dissolving everything that exists, and while all that is happening, He is either revealing or concealing Himself as the source of all diversity. We experience the first three acts in every moment of our lives. Everything lasts for a while and then is gone, including our physical body. It was created, we do our best to maintain it, and at some point it fails. What's important in this cycle is whether we have revealed the source of this life as our own Self, or whether we have continued to conceal the source of both our body and our individuated existence.

Grace is synomymous with the power of revelation. Because we are conscious and have the self-reflective capacity to know our own state, we can choose revelation instead of concealment. In every moment of life, regardless of what is arising and subsiding, we get to decide whether our experience is about revealing our higher nature or concealing it. Revealing happens if we are using the triadic powers of will, knowledge, and action to discover our source. Conversely, concealing is the result of using those same powers to serve ourselves, which only perpetuates our limitation and separation. That's why it is so powerful to understand that God's powers of creation are *our* powers of creation—our powers to create and choose our experience in this life.

grace is another word for revelation

It is through Śiva's five powers that manifestation takes place, and although the *tattvas* describe this as the descent of Consciousness, we have the choice to ascend back through those

same levels of awareness and discover their infinite source. This is the purpose of our life and of our spiritual practice: to see through God's emission and multiplicity so that we can achieve union with our own divine source. Our self-reflective capacity is the gift we have received from Śiva. It enables us to recognize who we really are. We see the light that is always present within us and choose to engage in whatever practices are needed to fully uncover that light.

Since the world is the reflection of the Divine, we should think of it as the field in which our *sādhana* becomes a means to understanding unity. We experience the world, and even our own lives, as separate from ourselves because we perceive everything in terms of subject and object. By looking for the non-difference between subject and object we eliminate the perspective of differentiation—the very definition of duality. This is really a discussion of Consciousness (the subject or knower) and the objects that can be perceived by the knower. The appearance of an object is always dependent on Consciousness. Objects have no autonomy in themselves but exist only because they are *known* to exist. All of life is the projection of Consciousness, held within unity. If we see and experience anything as separate from Consciousness, we are functioning from dualistic awareness.

In our spiritual practice we seek to make contact with God, the supreme subject who is never separate from any object because all objects are known *as Himself*. Only from that depth of consciousness can we see the limitation of our own perspective. We begin to recognize that our thoughts and definitions of ourselves are always in terms of a separation between subject and object—and this leads us to experience that joy or sorrow is created from something outside of us. Our *sādhana* should bring us in contact with the fullness and completeness that shatters the illusion that we are, by nature, a finite and separate being. Immersed in our true Self, the supreme subject, we discover the effulgent joy of our own existence instead of being imprisoned in ignorance. Consciousness needs no object.

THE VEILS OF DUALITY

In order to fully ascend to higher consciousness, we must pierce through three fundamental veils of duality that limit our experience. The *tattvas* speak of these as "impurities," although I typically refer to them as "veils." They are:

- The impurity/veil of individuality (I am separate)— which limits freedom and awareness of Consciousness. When divine will is limited in us, we think we are in control.

- The impurity/veil of *māyā* (I am different)—which gives rise to diversity and relative distinctions. This limits our knowledge of the Self.

- The impurity/veil of action (I am the doer)—which is the limitation of God's agency of action. It binds the individual to the results of action and obscures the infinite (pure) powers of will, knowledge, and action.

We have to transcend the experience of these veils—I am separate from God, I am different from God, and I am doing something—because liberation requires that we live from a new place in ourselves. Liberation is the direct experience of "I am Śiva." That realization only happens when we are freed from the part of us that *doesn't* know we are God. If you are seeking the highest experience in life, serving the Divine is the means to discover that truth. Having this higher awareness is worth all the pain and sacrifice involved in spiritual growth. It's worth offering all the pettiness that we call our life into the fire of Consciousness.

To aid you in finding this resonance of service and surrender within you, I suggest you now practice the guided meditation entitled *Mahā Mantra*. (You will find a link to a free download of all the mantra meditations in this book in Appendix B, page 303.) This meditation will help tune you in to the part of you that truly wishes to surrender into a life of unconditional service to God. In this meditation we also explore the internal breath, the absolute stillness that resides in the center of the *suṣumṇa* (sushumna). When we find that deepest consciousness in ourselves, we discover that we do not even need the physical breath to be alive. We are being breathed by God.

SERVICE FREES US FROM NEED

When we have a profound inner experience, we are naturally filled with gratitude and wish to serve that which gave us life. But we must actively choose to serve unconditionally. Only you can choose whether to serve God or to serve yourself—but understand that there is no such thing as non-selfless service. We choose service as our *sādhana* precisely *because* it frees us from self-focused awareness.

For service to be truly selfless and about giving, we must free ourselves from any thoughts of "I need this and I want that." The fundamental reason people are not free is that they will not move past their belief that they need. Śiva doesn't say, "I need." He simply says, "I am." Need arises from the veil of duality that asserts our separation, because as long as we feel separate from God, we will remain incomplete. Furthermore, we will not use our conscious choice to discover the place in us that has no need, because we are so attached to the idea that we do need something. We end up so busy pursuing our needs that we forget to look for the fullness and effulgence within us that is complete in itself.

Not being complete is the primary effect of being separate from one's own Self. We translate incompleteness into the need for this thing or person, or that ideal situation. The real problem is that need always escalates as we believe our experience of lack and pursue the same things again and again. The very pursuit of need, in fact, reinforces our need, because we do feel incomplete. Searching for something to complete us, we perpetually look for something that can never do it. Never.

For service to be truly selfless and about giving, we must free ourselves from any thoughts of "i need this and i want that"

This endless pursuit reinforces the endless pursuit. Every one of us has had the same experience: This person or that dynamic didn't fulfill our needs. We get hooked into thinking that the next person or situation will be "the one." There's a message here! And so much of the time it is our incessant resonance of demand that somebody else complete us, that sets them up for failure. They cannot do it, because the only part of us that can function above all levels of need is already full. So instead of examining whether someone can fulfill your need, aggressively pursue inner fullness. Once you've done that, your relationships with people will completely change. Whether they do or do not fulfill some need doesn't change your experience in yourself, or even your experience with them. Because let's be honest, when we don't get what we want from others, we close to them.

Seva frees us of need. It will change your life. Every time you start contracting, thinking, "I am not getting what I want," stop immediately and start opening and giving. We're like four-year-olds with toys. You give a kid a birthday present, and for thirty seconds this new treasure is the most important thing in the world . . . and then they're looking for the next gift.

seva frees us of need. you have been given everything you need: consciousness and the capacity to know yourself

Let me make this clear. You have already received. You have been given everything you need: consciousness and the capacity to know yourself. You've unwrapped the present, yet you insist, "That's not what I wanted." God has given you life. What else could you want? If you can simply feel the joy in your own existence then all the struggle will be gone. I don't mean put aside. I mean gone. What do you want in this life? The same things you've been pursuing lifetime after lifetime that have only caused suffering? Try something new. Every time you think you have a need that's not fulfilled, turn around and serve.

Do not enter into a life of seva if you're not willing to let go of what you think you need. Do not enter into seva out of need. Why bother? As Rudi would say, that would be such a sad reward for all that hard work. You must be willing to discover what seva means. Only a rare person knows what it truly means and still steps through that door. At least become a person who does enter into service without thought of price. Along the way, you will discover what it means. You will be thrown into that fire of Consciousness, and you will be both the oblation and the fire that burns the offering. Your choice to serve God is your self-reflective decision.

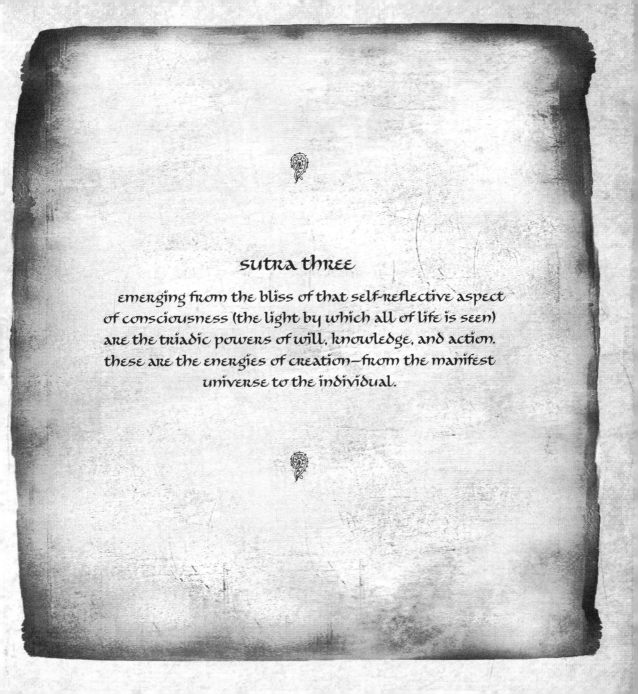

sutra three

emerging from the bliss of that self-reflective aspect
of consciousness (the light by which all of life is seen)
are the triadic powers of will, knowledge, and action.
these are the energies of creation—from the manifest
universe to the individual.

The potential for creation inherently exists within Consciousness. The previous sutra stated that Śiva looks back at Himself with His five faces, and He doesn't need to do anything in order to experience His own state. But He does choose to express that effulgence, to let His bliss flow out. Within Śiva, bliss is simply divine light, and from this space manifestation takes place. Out of the interplay between Consciousness and bliss, *prakāśa* and *vimarśa*, the will to create emits itself and rolls out as knowledge and action. The goddess Parā (will) is therefore depicted as being above Parāparā (knowledge) and Aparā (action), although these energies are essentially inseparable. Because all of creation arises from Śiva's power of will, Anuttara Trika traditionally says there is only one goddess—only Parā.

Look again at the *tattva* chart in Appendix C, page 304. Śiva's first five powers are listed at the top: *cit śakti* (Consciousness), *ānanda śakti* (bliss), *icchā śakti* (will), *jñāna śakti* (knowledge), and *kriyā śakti* (action). In the chart, these powers are placed above a gray line, which is Śiva's next power, called *māyā*. *Māyā* is equal to the five powers in the sense that it is the veil of limitation that creates the appearance of duality and obscures higher awareness. This is where separation takes place—but remember, from Śiva's perspective *māyā* is the *veil* of duality, not the *reality* of duality. In the descent of Consciousness, Śiva's unified awareness is held within everything, all the way down the chart, to the level of rocks.

It is really *vimarśa*, the self-reflective capacity, that gets contracted as Consciousness descends. When the power of *vimarśa* is concealed, limited understanding arises because the individual cannot perceive himself to be infinite Consciousness. We can also look at *māyā* in the context of Śiva's fivefold acts— creation, maintenance, dissolution, concealing, and revealing. *Māyā* is the concealing force, but penetrating back through *māyā* reveals that we are not separate or different from Śiva's unlimited powers.

Even though we arise from God and are never separate from Him, inherent in our experience is the likelihood that we may not realize our status. Instead of knowing, "I am an individuated expression of God," we may feel, "I am an individual who's separate from God." There is a critical difference between those two perspectives because the first points us back up toward Śiva's unlimited powers, while the other leads us down into further misunderstanding. We have to choose which road to take.

Consciousness itself permeates all manifestation. Śiva always knows He's one light, but He creates the veil of *māyā* to produce the misunderstanding that the light has broken into parts. Once the power of *māyā* is in place, to complicate matters further, Śiva decides to play even more tricks on us. Śiva takes *māyā*, *tattva* 6,

from shiva's perspective maya is the veil of duality, not the reality of duality

and filters it through *tattvas* 7 to 11. From omnipotence He creates limited ability, omnipresence turns into space, eternity becomes time, and so forth. It is only after all this obscuration happens that we as individual subjects are created at the level of *tattva* 12.

Why would Śiva place us in such a predicament? Because He values His own bliss and knowledge of Himself so highly that He's not going to make it easy for His creation to experience it! If it's too easy, we won't value it and we won't seek to achieve it. Just as in a child's game of hide and seek, the joy is in the discovery. In the "play of Consciousness" we get to find out that Śiva has been hiding in plain sight. Since we did not set up the rules of the game, we can stop blaming ourselves for not knowing that we are God. We were born in duality, in apparent separation from Śiva, and simply cannot understand unity from that state.

SHIVA'S POWERS ARE OUR OWN

We are not the first thing to manifest, yet the same, highest state of consciousness is available to us at any moment in our lives. To experience that, we must align our will with divine will, personified as the goddess Parā. By practicing the guided meditation *The Mantra of Will* (see Appendix B), we begin to do just that. We offer our will into God's will, and we attune to the grace of Parā through the mantra "*Oṃ sauḥ Parāyai namaḥ.*" (Note that "sauḥ" is pronounced "sauh-hoo.") In our meditation, and throughout our life, we ask to serve God's will rather than our own; to transmute the power we experience as ours into a higher power. In the discussion of future sutras I'll provide a similar meditation for the powers of knowledge and action, because these three powers always go hand in hand.

The *tattvas* categorize the first five powers as "pure awareness" simply because they exist within Śiva's own Consciousness as potentiality—not as form or manifestation but as one unity. We are here to serve that One, and although this may take the form of serving people, we are really only serving God. It is through serving the powers of Śiva that we come to experience them as pure awareness. We begin to know "I am Śiva." From that understanding we recognize that although Śiva's powers are our powers, and we can do what we want with them, we ultimately don't *need* to do anything. The transformation of our limited experience of those powers into the unlimited experience of them creates freedom.

The three powers of will, knowledge, and action determine everything we think, do, act, reject, attack, etcetera. These energies are always expressed through our own perspective and we have to work to penetrate through our interpretation of them because we perpetually misunderstand. We think that they are only our powers, and we therefore assume they are limited. We don't experience them as God's unlimited powers.

DIVERSITY BECOMES DUALITY

Tattvas 12 through 16 delineate how and why, as we experience and misunderstand our individuality, we further perpetuate the experience of separateness and objectivity. Our capacity for self-reflection is dissipated by everything we see and interact with, and we define ourselves by our experience of diversity. Although Śiva knows that everything is part of Himself, we only perceive separate things. There's "me" and there's "it." The universal, pure, supreme subject identifies with objectivity, something outside itself. The intellect, the ego, and the mind are what we use to try to define and understand that experience of separateness.

The problem, of course, is that we get locked in these levels of awareness and can only perceive duality. This is why we need a spiritual practice. It is why we have to serve in order to break through the confines of our own experience. We see, hear, and think. We have a body, we want sex and food. These are all normal aspects of being a human being, but they may limit our awareness.

You could say that everything below the level of *tattva* 12 is simply part of how life functions. But when our awareness rises back up to the vantage point of *tattva* 12, we engage in life and understand our experience not as a separate individuated entity but as an individuated expression of God. That is a critical juncture in every spiritual person's life.

Will, knowledge, and action are called Parā, Parāpara, and Apara because all energies are goddesses. We can engage those powers from our limited understanding, thereby concealing their highest nature, or we can engage them in order to reveal the unlimited capacity of those energies. If we shift in this way, we understand that these higher levels of consciousness are available to us. We've been given the gift of these three powers and the question is always: How are we going to use them? This decision is the crux of *tattva* 12. It is the crux of individuality.

Since we *do* get bogged down in duality, we must make the choice to rise above the smallness of daily life. Stop struggling with all of life's struggles. Stop fighting in and about your relationships. Stop succumbing to the limited needs of being an individuated, misunderstood person, and begin to focus your awareness on knowing the truth instead of perpetuating that which is not true. We have to consciously turn away from being embroiled in struggle and choose to move up. It's only our direct experience that makes spiritual growth real. Otherwise we think liberation is just a fantasy, because our experience to date disproves any higher reality. We can't know what's "up there" if we don't see for ourselves. If you're stuck and not sure how to rise through all your stuff, take out a pick-axe and make a hole. Spirit has no form. You just go up.

we must make the choice to rise above the smallness of daily life. stop struggling with all of life's struggles

We can either accept our ignorance—ignorance being the term for not knowing ourselves, not knowing the truth—or we can demand, "There's got to be more to life than this!" What's most important is that we stop looking outside ourselves to have that experience. When we are stuck in our false sense of incompleteness, we continue to bind ourselves. This happens because we cling to the perception that the world is outside us. We seek to own material objects or try to change people in an attempt to find completeness in a realm that can never complete us. We continue to function in the field of limited action to get and keep those things or situations we desire. By focusing on external reality, we engage in action that limits our capacity to know, and we end up abusing the people we say we love.

The amazing thing about duality is that it is as infinite on its own level as infinite awareness is. There is no edge of duality that we fall off. You just keep going and going and going, and the further you go out, the further you are from your center. We become like those domestic pigs who, when let out into the wild, revert to being wild boars. They lose their "civilized" nature, grow tusks, and grow coarse hair all over their bodies. This is what happens to us. The more we fight with life, the more we behave like animals, fighting to survive and to get what we want.

THE POWER OF GRACE TO AWAKEN US

We get so lost in duality that we not only forget we are divine, we even stop looking for our divinity. The mind always functions as a device of the ego, which adamantly believes in its separateness and fights to defend this conception of itself. The ego thinks, "I am this, I am that," forgetting its true nature to the extent that it no longer tries to find what that is. Fortunately, grace has already awakened something in each of us that says, "I am in you, find Me." This is the power of grace, that it can reach into everyone's hearts and create the longing to know God—to know that there is no duality, nothing outside our own infinite Self. Our job is to respond to that grace instead of getting caught in the struggles of life, which are only the surface reverberations of our separation from God.

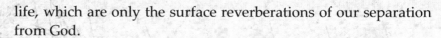

These *tattvas* are talking about human experience, about whether we choose to discover our divinity or continue to live within the limited perspective of duality. As we understand Śiva's supreme powers and how they become limited, we start to have a new perspective on our lives. We can locate our own awareness in that hierarchy of levels of consciousness outlined in the *tattvas*. Mostly, we stop looking at our tensions and patterns as those *things* we get caught in, and instead recognize them as contractions of consciousness, i.e., energy not in motion. Life is simply energy, and our own tensions are energies that are contracted and stagnant. If we can take whatever density we are experiencing—guilt, shame, self-rejection, hatred, attacking, reacting—and put them into flow, then we no longer have to battle through our issues on their own level.

Remember, we get to choose whether to experience ourselves as individuated expressions of God or as individuals separate from God. We decide to ascend to higher consciousness instead of letting consciousness continue to descend. What's amazing is that when we talk about the arising of creation, we think of it as the *expansion* of consciousness. Out of Śiva's mere Presence, the whole universe was created. In reality, consciousness is *descending* into form—not expanding, not rising. Multiplicity is created but as soon as that happens, the experience is of two . . . of three . . . of billions . . . and Śiva's highest, undifferentiated Consciousness is concealed in form.

The meditation accompanying this sutra includes the practice of extending our awareness to *dvādaśānta* because that is the abode of Parā, Parāparā, and Aparā, the goddesses of Śiva's will, knowledge, and action. This is the space in which you were manifested. Like a drop emerging from an eyedropper, your individuality descends out of Śiva's supreme powers. These are not only the energies from which we are created, but they are also located within our own psychic system. We find the lotus filament in our *suṣumṇa* and follow it as it rises through the density of the contraction of consciousness, up into pure Consciousness.

In our meditation, we have the experience of moving back up to *dvādaśānta*, but that isn't an end point. It's a beginning, the supreme *bindu* between individuality and divinity. You cannot take your possessions or your tensions through that door. Only spirit moves through it, and all individuality is merged back into infinite identity in that space. Experiencing Śiva's powers within *dvādaśānta* is what Rudi called "the spiritual horizontal." Exploring that space further extends our awareness of infinite Consciousness, of Śiva Himself.

The essence of Consciousness is bliss, out of which emerges Śiva's will to express His state. His outward breath creates the diversification of the One and His in-breath the unification of the many. These are the two movements of dynamic stillness, the arising and subsiding of all life. The outward breath of God is empowered by His will to express freedom, embedded in His knowledge that He is always all things, simply manifesting the plurality of divine forms on the screen of His own Consciousness.

we find the lotus filament in our sushumna and follow it as it rises through the density of the contraction of consciousness, up into pure consciousness

The inward breath of God is how He draws back into Himself all those powers to rest in the bliss of His own undifferentiated existence. Each of us is alive because of this pulsation of Śiva's supreme awareness. That is why we can say, in every sense, that we are being breathed by God. We should all be so lucky as to live in the joy of simply being breathed. When we understand that Śiva descends and manifests solely to expand His own joy and freedom, our direct experience gives us feedback about how close or how far we are from aligning our will with Śiva's will. Are you having what Śiva's having, or are you experiencing something less? Have you chosen to be free or to perpetuate pain?

rudi said, "within a human being, the wish is the most powerful force that exists"

This discussion is presented in the context of seva because only in serving can we change our perspective. We are blind because we're constantly focusing on our own needs, in a constant search for completeness in a realm that can never satisfy. We want to have the experience of unity, of knowing that all that exists is God. If you truly want that, offer your life in service. Offer your life in service to that which gave you life. Offer your life into discovering the truth about yourself. And in that process you will mostly discover every untruth about yourself.

Rudi said, "Within a human being, the wish is the most powerful force that exists." You get anything you want. The question is: What is your wish? Use your self-reflective awareness. Shine a light on yourself to know whether you are functioning within the limited constraints of Śiva's powers or are sacrificing all limitations into the unwavering wish to allow those energies to express themselves through you as supreme powers.

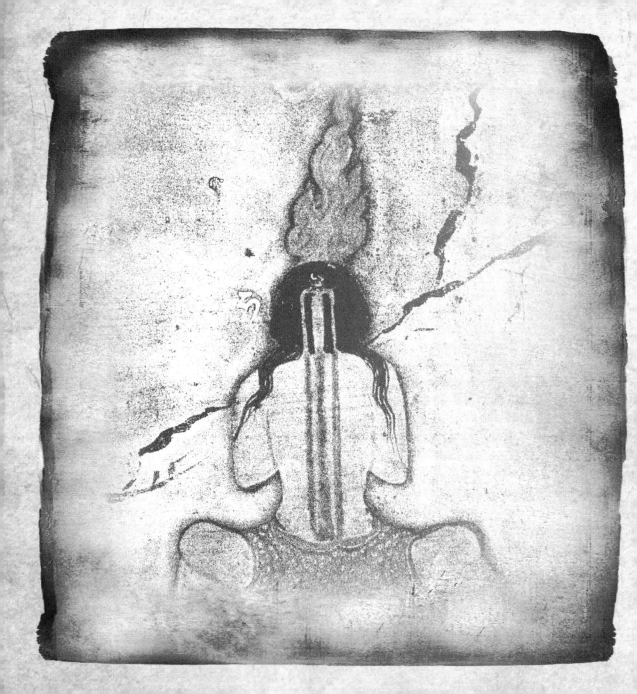

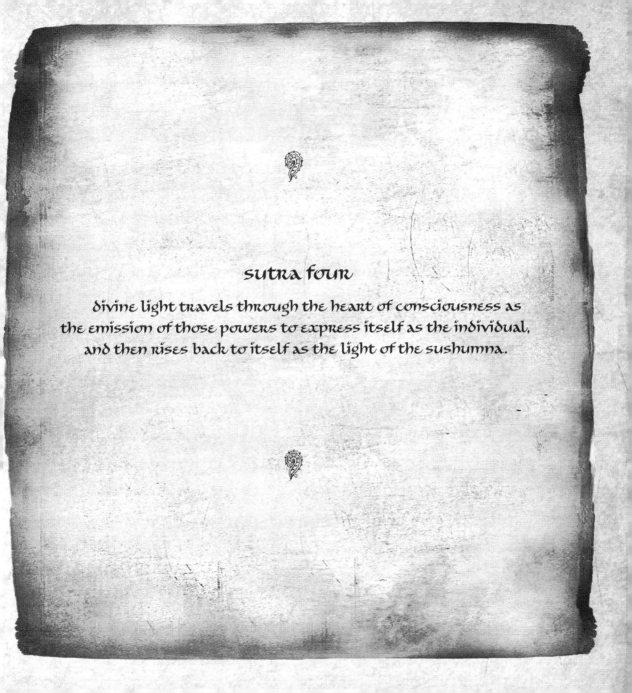

sutra four

divine light travels through the heart of consciousness as
the emission of those powers to express itself as the individual,
and then rises back to itself as the light of the sushumna.

All of Śiva's powers pass through *dvādaśānta*, the abode of the goddess Parā. We've seen that Śiva creates those energies from within His power of Consciousness, to express the joy of His own existence. The infinitesimally infinite *bindu* point *dvādaśānta*—which is above, below, inside, and outside us—is where we manifest. That is why teachers in the nondual Tantric tradition emphasize that bringing our awareness to *dvādaśānta* is the pathway back to our own source.

There's a beautiful line in the Yoginī Hṛdayam, an eleventh-century Tantric text, which says, "Recognize the goddess as pure light, which emanates and creates from within the *suṣumṇa* and creates you." This was how that wisdom was expressed a thousand years ago. In his book *Stillness*, Charles Ridley offers a similar description in the language of modern technology. I'm going to paraphrase it a bit:

Modern medicine has now demonstrated that in the first two weeks following conception, the embryo possesses no structure but is simply a clear-as-glass, liquid crystal matrix. Then on day fourteen, it begins to organize cells that produce a visible line in the embryo, called the primitive streak or the midline [the *suṣumṇa*]. The core of that midline is stillness or Presence enfolded within that electromagnetic energy field, and it is from that field that the development of the human being takes place. From this primitive streak of light, an invisible line transforms into a visible line and becomes the core around which a human creates himself. Arising out of that streak of light, like branches from a tree trunk, emerge all the aspects of a human being. Essentially, the progression is from the original primitive streak of invisible stillness, an imminence of light, which turns into manifest form.

the definitive description of kundalini centers around the fact that we are an individuated expression of the divine

Today, this can be seen under a microscope, but the ancient Tantrics saw it through the lens of their own awareness. How amazing.

KUNDALINI: THE VITAL FORCE IN THE SUSHUMNA

The definitive description of *kuṇḍalinī* centers around the fact that we are an individuated expression of the Divine. The five powers of Śiva, particularly the three powers of will, knowledge, and action, manifest as the vital force within our *suṣumṇa*. This is *kuṇḍalinī*, the goddess Parā, giving rise to us. In the tradition of Śrī Vidyā, a later extension out of the practice of Anuttara Trika, Parā is called Lalitā or Tripurasundarī. As an individuated expression of Śiva's will, you exist *as* and *because* of her energy.

Parā's energy resides in the *suṣumṇa* (the central channel in our psychic body), and in the *iḍā* and *piṅgala* (the two major channels that crisscross the *suṣumṇa*). By bringing our attention to this vital force in us we activate it, allowing it to rise through the *suṣumṇa* and back to Consciousness, in what Nityananda called "the heart-space"—the chakras in the heart, center of the head, and the top of the head. The *suṣumṇa* is in the subtle body, thinner than the filament of a lotus stalk. That's why you often see *kuṇḍalinī* described as the flowering of a thousand-petaled lotus. The lotus represents unmanifest Consciousness, held up by the stalk of the *suṣumṇa*, created from within itself out of the vitality that gives it life. A lotus flower is not floating in space. It's connected to its own source, which isn't the water or even the mud at the bottom of the pond, but to energy itself.

There are three aspects of *kuṇḍalinī*, depicted as three coils of a snake. Her head is turned around and folded down on herself, to show that she is dormant within us. In reality, she only appears to be asleep because we are unaware of her and haven't yet awakened her power. *Sādhana* is that awakening, and the awakening agent is usually *śaktipāta* (shaktipat)—the direct transmission of spiritual force from a teacher—which allows *kuṇḍalinī's* energy to start to stir. As her eyes open and she uncoils, she rises back through the *suṣumṇa*, eating every obstacle in sight as she ascends back to God.

The three facets of *kuṇḍalinī* express different energies within us. *Parā kuṇḍalinī* is the power of our spiritual self, the primal streak of light. *Parā* also means "highest." The next coil is *cit kuṇḍalinī*, the power of the mind and emotions. The third is *prāṇa kuṇḍalinī*, the power that gives life to the physical body. It's important to understand that it is not *your* breath that gives life to your body, but rather, that you are being breathed by Parā. Held within the center of the *suṣumṇa* is her power, expressed as the internal breath, animating all three levels of our existence.

We're alive not because we're breathing but because *kuṇḍalinī* has given us existence. *Kuṇḍalinī* is the divine light of Śiva's Consciousness, His own self-awareness, expressed through His powers of creation for only one purpose: to expand joy and freedom. Śiva's powers of will, knowledge, and action are the powers of our psychic body, and that's why, in our meditation, we can use our breath to bring our awareness inside, away from apparent external duality, to access those powers within.

THE PRACTICE OF AWAKENING KUNDALINI

We have the choice to share in Śiva's unconditional joy and freedom or to live in a limited state. Our expression of *kuṇḍalinī's* power binds us if we extend it without self-knowledge, but it frees us when we allow it to ascend back to its source, the home of all self-knowledge. As Abhinavagupta said a thousand years ago, "There is no other divine fire able to consume the whole of duality than *kuṇḍalinī*."

Abhinavagupta was a great Tantric master who looked back into centuries of teachings and extracted the essence of their knowledge, which he called Anuttara Trika. Anuttara means "none higher," an apt name for what Abhinavagupta described in the Tantrāloka as the highest practice available to humans in their attempt to reach God. My own lineage and practice of Kuṇḍalī

Sādhana stems from that tradition. All our inner work, including the double-breath exercise, opening our hearts, and establishing ourselves in the flow within the *suṣumṇa*, gives us access to the highest awareness available to us in the space of *dvādaśānta*.

Parā kuṇḍalinī is the power of God's will that gives us life by expressing herself as the *suṣumṇa*. It is who we are. Our choice is to either direct our energy and consciousness back into the *suṣumṇa* or allow it to project outward. If we choose to internalize our life force we must take our energy out of manifestation and the appearance of duality. We bring our awareness out of the mind, pull it back into the light of the *suṣumṇa*, and channel all energy into the flow within us. By reconnecting to that vital force, we create the opening for the expansion and ascent of consciousness, allowing all energy to be absorbed back into its own source.

para kundalini is the power of god's will that gives us life by expressing herself as the sushumna

As this energy moves up through the *suṣumṇa*, it opens all the chakras, dissolving the *granthi* at the base of the spine, in the heart, and in the center of the head. These *granthi* are the coalescence of misunderstanding and the tension created from that misunderstanding. That energy gets condensed to the point where it functions like a granite cover, blocking the light in our subtle body. Only the vital force in the *suṣumṇa* can dissolve that density, piercing through and dissipating these caps of darkness, thereby allowing its own energy to ascend back to God. This is the power of Kuṇḍalinī Sādhana.

The maturation of our consciousness must include our capacity to be still, and to focus our awareness deep enough and

long enough to allow the awakening of *kuṇḍalinī* to uncover that higher awareness. What really happens is that we are consuming our misunderstanding and all dualistic experience. If we wish this to happen, we have to surrender. We have to be willing to be changed, without thought of price, by the energy that is arising in us. That's why it is understood, when engaging in any practice that focuses on the awakening of *kuṇḍalinī*, that we rouse her, get out of the way, and let her do what she's going to do. If you start resisting what *she* wants to do to free you, you will suffer.

In reality, you will probably suffer anyway as this tremendous force opens in you and destroys everything you believed to be true about yourself! This is why we must surrender. We ask, "May my will be Your will," "May I know You as my Self," and, "May all my actions serve You." Don't ask if you don't want it, but here's the kicker: part of you wants it and part of you doesn't. That's a given—don't beat yourself up about it. You have the capacity to know what you're choosing, so choose the part of you that wants it. In its highest form, the part of you that wants it is not "you." It is the descent of grace within you, demanding that you wake up. We interpret this as, "I wish to awaken."

We have already received this grace. We were given life as well as the opportunity to know the source of that life through our spiritual practice. From your perspective it may seeem that your decision to begin a spiritual practice was based on a desire to end suffering. It's not. It's because the highest aspect of you wants to be free. Surrender to that wish to come home. Surrender your will—which reinforces the ego's wish to *not* be free—into

we have to be willing to be changed, without thought of price, by the energy that is arising in us

Śiva's will, which is always the expansion of freedom. We let God's will express itself through us, as us, and we even witness it being expressed as the people around us.

KNOWING OURSELVES

One of the veils of duality is the belief "I am the doer." In reality, not only are we *not* doing anything, but we have to be willing to let something be done to us. Śiva is the only doer. There's a lot of New Age talk about "co-creation" with God. This is nonsense. Let's see, there's God in all His infinite power, and there's me, and I'm going to co-create. What is that really saying? I'm going to get God to create what I want. I'm going to get God to give me what I think I need instead of finding the place in me that is free and established in absolute unconditionality.

By truly understanding the *Mantra of Knowledge*, "May I know You as my Self," we begin to fall into the experience of "I am Śiva." (See Appendix B.) We penetrate through the misunderstanding of what we think life is and who we think we are, proactively sending the email, "Dear God, please let me know You as my Self. Please free me from the belief that I am separate from You, that I am anything other than You." Ironically, when we open our hearts and deeply ask for understanding, the first thing that happens is that we see reflected back on ourselves, moment after moment, all of our *misunderstanding* of who we think we are.

If our wish is to know ourselves, our experience of engaging with all of life has to become radically different. No longer can that interaction be created out of our projection of misunderstanding. We have to clearly see what everything is. How can we understand something if we're immediately projecting what we think we know, based on our limited awareness? How could we understand the truth of it? Look at anything, even a rag. We fight to the death to prove it's a piece of cloth. What is it really? Energy! That doesn't deny that it's also a rag, but it's not the truth about what it is. This is what we do with life. We project what we think it is, based on our experience to date, and then we defend our position.

What do you want in this life? To know the truth, or to defend yours? There is another New Age saying, "I need to speak my truth." Why not speak God's truth? We engage in a million "truths" a day. The image we create of ourselves, the projections we make on everyone around us—they're all true, because we invented them! That doesn't mean they're the highest truth. Authentic *sādhakas* seek to have everything they think they know disproved, and there is no level of spiritual practice in which that maxim does not apply.

If we're sincerely willing to serve God, we discover the willingness to let go of our limited perspective. God's powers are embedded in us, in our psychic body, in our *suṣumnā*. As we align our will with God's will, we work to clear the path in our psychic mechanism that allows *kuṇḍalinī* to rise and devour all untruths. When the heart chakra expands into the chakras in the center and the top of the head and up into the space of *dvādaśānta*, everything we think and feel, and every action we take, reflect Śiva's powers

authentic sadhakas seek to have everything they think they know disproved, and there is no level of spiritual practice in which that maxim does not apply

being expressed through our individuality. The awakening of *kuṇḍalinī* means that the authentic *sādhaka* is consciously raising the level from which he or she acts within those powers.

We transition from our limited, individual perspective to allowing ourselves to understand and function from the level of God's infinite powers, before duality covered the light. Because divinity has already contracted into individuality we must work to reverse the act of concealment, to expand our contracted consciousness back to its fullness. God manifests us through the powers of His own emission, and our personal experience should reflect the knowledge that we're created as an individuated expression of that same divine power. Think about what your life would be like if you experienced yourself as the vehicle for Śiva to display His unlimited power and truth. This is liberation.

If you want to go into another room, don't try to walk through the wall. You'll end up with a concussion and won't get there. Why not just open the door? Tantric practices tell us that the only way to God is through the *suṣumṇa*. As our energy rises, it exposes and consumes all dualistic thinking, until every facet of diversity is experienced as one thing, not two. Liberation is freedom from misunderstanding, and you must burn it in the fire of your own consciousness. It doesn't matter what misunderstanding it is, or what level it functions in. Throw it all into the sacrificial fire.

It only takes one moment of truth, one moment of offering yourself like you really mean it—like it has something to do with your own life. Otherwise, at the end of your life you might regret that you didn't make the right choice in that one moment. Don't be left with only regret. When you do offer yourself, the depth of change you need to make becomes apparent. It may seem to be a daunting task, given the misunderstandings you have created in this life. So just ask, "God give me the strength to truly change." In reality, God already gave you the strength. Will you use it to transform your life? Only you get to choose. No one else can choose for you.

sutra five

hold fast to the lamp of sadhana and your own
light will merge with the universal light shining
forth to illuminate the perfection of your life.

This sutra emphasizes the power of our wish to grow, our wish to know the God who dwells within us. It's said that the difference between "good" and "great" is discipline, and that maxim certainly applies to our *sādhana*. Our spiritual discipline is exhibited in the conscious choices we make moment by moment, because this is what dictates our experience. Paradoxically, from within our own consciousness, we ourselves create the situations in which we have to make those choices. We create dynamics that appear to be "out there," or different than us, so that we can choose to discover unity in those apparent differences.

Every act we perform must be in search of the knowledge that we determine our own experience. Everything we encounter is designed by us to illuminate the perfection of our life, to show us that none of those conditions have the power to change our experience unless we allow them to do so. Whether it's a major attraction or a horrible repulsion, it's all just our minds deciding that one thing is good, another is bad. We think, "This is a condition I like, that is a condition I don't like." These ideas are the expression of duality, and they lead to suffering.

Buddha, too, experienced that life is suffering. But then he sat down, touched the earth, and said, "I will not move from here until I am free of suffering." In response to that declaration all the demons, all earthly temptations, arose before him. Beautiful women were dancing, music was playing, wine was flowing, gargoyles appeared. This plethora of distraction amounted to a powerful test of his resolve, demanding, "Are you serious about your wish?" And what did Buddha do? He got quieter, stiller, remaining firm in his conviction until every one of those apparitions disappeared.

Tantric tradition unequivocally states that our experience of life—and all of the apparent diversity and suffering that happen because of that experience—is our doorway to unity. But in order to walk through that door, we must approach every experience from a higher consciousness than we normally function from: not from our mind, which is constantly trying to define experience, but from the awareness of an open heart that simply recognizes the perfection of life as part of the totality.

joy is not created out of form or diminished by it

THE POWER OF A DISCIPLINED WISH

Be like Buddha. Hold fast to your wish, and every time someone, something, some thought or emotion starts to take your energy away from your choice, say "No, I will not accept this as my life. I choose to be happy." Joy is not created out of form or diminished by it. Use your wish to find that unconditional joy in yourself, to live in the effulgence of your own existence. Do not accept anything less. This is the power of a disciplined wish. Don't let your resolve succumb to the mind, to thoughts like, "I would grow if I didn't have so many things in my life that get in the way." Your wish must roar like a lion, and it must be expressed in everything you think and do.

Talk is cheap. The wish to grow will be tested whenever we need to open bigger, and there is nothing that pries open our hearts faster than service. We ask to give, again and again, so that we get bigger than our ego, bigger than any conditions we might face. The same dynamic can either cause suffering or be the opportunity for service. We only expand and deepen our awareness by opening our heart beyond whatever density we encounter. We can't get bigger from the mind because the mind is what created that contraction in the first place.

In the Bhagavad Gītā, Kṛṣṇa says to Arjuna, "Among thousands, only a few strive to attain perfection. And of those who strive, only a few know Me in truth." What distinguishes those few from the thousands? Rudi built his entire freedom on one simple concept, the transmuting of his wish into God's wish. The amount of discipline, clarity, and conviction that you bring to your wish is the determining factor in whether that wish frees you, or you end up living a life of regret.

Understand that no person or situation can affect the power of your wish. No condition can steal your freedom unless you let it. Your wish is forged in the fire of your own conviction, in the face of your own suffering. Are you going to continue living in that suffering or free yourself from it? We can easily get caught in all of the details that, like legal documents, obfuscate the real cause of our problem. Or, we can penetrate through the perpetual hubbub of activity and discover where it all comes from. The essence of *sādhana* is finding the doorway to the source of that diversity and activity, and we can only locate that portal in our heart. True understanding is not in somebody else's consciousness; it's in our own.

Sādhana is the expansion of consciousness. Lamenting about the current state of your awareness is useless. Just hold on to your wish to truly live in a state of simplicity and joy. When you see yourself engaging in confusion, reinforcing your tensions and projections and creating suffering in yourself, stop doing it. Take a breath, draw it inside, and find the place that breath came from. Find that deeper awareness, and don't give up until you see God clearly. What is so important that you would choose not to do that? Sex? Power? Making a million dollars? That list is endless.

In many ways, our essential choice is black and white. It *is* that profoundly simple. Choose to find happiness within instead of endlessly pursuing it, trying to locate completeness everywhere but where it really exists. As long as we feel incomplete we will perpetually look for one thing or another to fill us. If this thing doesn't work, then the next will. We don't stop to consider what we've already been given—the freedom granted to us by God's will. We doubt the supreme will that gave us this life, our consciousness, and the capacity to choose. We doubt that God gave us freedom. All doubt is cancer and it will kill you. Love frees everything it touches.

all doubt is cancer and it will kill you. love frees everything it touches

RESISTANCE IS FUTILE

It's really Śiva's will that propels our life and our focus on freedom. But He also gives us the choice. "Do with Me as you wish" is Śiva's offering to us as well as our possible response to Him. Too often, we get caught in a tug-of-war, with Śiva on one side trying to pull us toward higher consciousness, while we're struggling to pull away. At some point we realize that's futile. We stop trying to sustain the same experience we've been having and ask for a different experience. Our life is a projection on the screen of our own consciousness. What it looks and feels like is always a reflection of where we function from. If we're perpetually making contact with the pain, suffering, and misunderstanding in ourselves then that's the reason we have that same experience as we engage the world. So we consciously choose to surrender our own experience of life to discover something deeper.

We keep surrendering our tensions, patterns, and needs until we tune out of those things long enough to see that all that has only been sustaining our separation from God. Despite knowing there's a God inside, we've been engaging a dimension in us that is holding on to separation. This is the definition of functioning from the ego. To change, we let go of our previous impressions, look for a different resonance, and then, as Rudi put it, it's a matter of depth over time. Extending that inner experience out into our life takes discipline and choice. So we begin to choose something different, repeat the mantra, do the meditation, and serve when we don't want to serve. I have found that the power of commitment is the most powerful energy within my own *sādhana*, and I have held on to that throughout the years. It is the commitment to service that really breaks down the barrier between inner and outer—because when you say, "I will serve You with my life," how can you back out of it?

Our meditation, our *sādhana*, our commitments, and our vows are all focusing our intention, focusing our will to uncover the experience of unity. The highest service we can do for God is to free ourselves. That's what He wants for us. So we use supreme will, as the power within us, to choose how we experience our own existence. If we don't have that conscious intention, the tensions, patterns, and impressions we carry from our karma will be what dictate our experience. We all know how powerful it feels to make things happen. Let's be *conscious* about what it is we're trying to have happen.

When you discover the place of wholeness in yourself then everything you engage in is part of that fulfillment. You can have everything in life, but if you lose sight of the one thing in your pursuit of everything, you're lost. Every day reflect: This is my life. Am I choosing the highest? Use your will to choose freedom. Choose simplicity, joy, and giving. If you live and serve from that perspective, you will very quickly transcend your focus on yourself. You will be focused on God and the perfection of life.

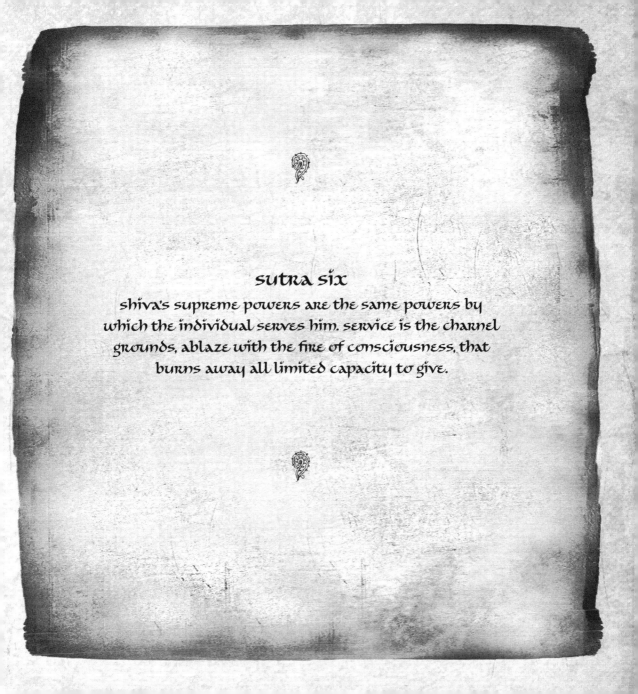

sutra six

shiva's supreme powers are the same powers by
which the individual serves him. service is the charnel
grounds, ablaze with the fire of consciousness, that
burns away all limited capacity to give.

So far we've had discussions about God's powers and how we can serve Him. Now, let's make it personal. Seva can be boiled down to one thing: giving what is wanted and needed and not what we want to give. Service will break down every boundary in you, every resistance to giving that you find surfacing in yourself. True selfless service is the conscious decision to discover and live in a state not affected by any condition or by what we are receiving or not receiving.

Śiva serves *us* unconditionally. I've said that "do with Me as you wish" describes His gift to each of us. God has given us life, and we have the will to do with it as we choose. Inherent in that relationship is the need to surrender our will so that we can do God's will. It's a reciprocal arrangement. We give up our limited understanding of who we are and what we want to do and instead begin doing what is asked of us. Regardless of who is asking us to serve, we know there is only one entity, one Consciousness doing the asking. We are always serving God—serving the freedom that already exists within us by opening to the divinity that is trying to express itself through us.

The decision to serve must be made from stillness, from a place that's capable of reflecting on what's really happening.

Otherwise we may resent all the disparate people who are always asking us to do this or that. Established in quietness, we view service from a different perspective, one of recognizing that God within us is creating the perfect situations for us to express our choice. Life does not happen to you—it happens from within you. Every dynamic that you find yourself in, every situation in which you have to decide whether to serve or not to serve, is created from within you to see if you meant what you asked for.

As we enter into this life of service, a number of issues arise, and one or the other tends to hook people. Some may ask, "You mean I have to surrender my action?" or, "I must surrender my will?" Another thinks, "If I have to give up everything, I won't know who I am!" It's endless. These questions are never separate, but we may focus on one or another at any given time, so let's look at some of the concerns people often have about service.

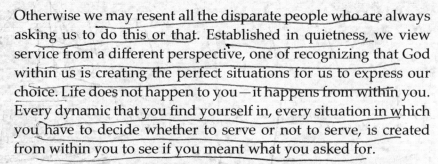

the fundamental thing about service is that we have to learn to give what we don't want to give

UNDERSTANDING HOW TO SERVE

The fundamental thing about service is that we have to learn to give what we don't want to give. We have to bypass all the excuses for not serving that crop up whenever we start analyzing if some action of ours is really what's wanted or not wanted. We don't get to judge other peoples' needs, because it's not really about *them*—it's about breaking down any internal resistance *we* have to simply serving. If we willingly give others what we *don't* want to give, we discover some very important things about ourselves.

Look at the people in your life who have a need. Where did they come from? Not from Topeka, Kansas. They came from within you! We create every dynamic to discover our own highest Self. We may think these people are "out there," continually demanding things of us—and they are—but we created them. In our response, we have to ask why we're doing an action. It's easy to get caught in: If you'll do it, I'll do it. If you'll open, I'll open. If you'll do this for me, I'll do that for you. Service is not tit for tat. It's about freeing ourselves from our need, from the unwillingness to give based on our own perspective.

We have to serve those who are closest to us, without trying to change them. Service is not displayed in grand gestures. You may have idealized concepts about going to Africa to feed the starving children, but before you buy that plane ticket, look at the people who are already in your life. Can you love and serve them unconditionally? Serving strangers is often easier than serving the people immediately surrounding us, because our nearest and dearest are the ones who push our buttons. So the next time your spouse or housemate leaves dirty dishes in the sink, look at your reaction. Does what they did shut you down, or can you rise above the situation and serve that person despite his/her faults?

If you're called to participate in social change, that's fine, but be sure you're not doing it to escape from the more difficult work of serving those who are already in your life, and never forget what it is you're attempting to do through service. Every government overthrown throughout history has been replaced with something equally bad, or even worse. It's always a question of what we're really trying to do with our life. I suggest that there is no higher service to God than freeing yourself.

SERVICE BREAKS DOWN OUR BOUNDARIES

Too often we think we can only serve when it doesn't cost us anything, but action is for the purpose of knowing our Self, and that includes the painful exposing of the parts of us that are closed. Serving unconditionally requires that we open our hearts without attachment to the results of action. That's the only way to get bigger than our limitations. Unfortunately, the mind always gets involved. We often come up with gross examples of how not to serve rather than getting quiet and asking how to truly respond. For example, students will ask a question like this: If a wino is sitting out on the street asking for money, should I give it to him? My answer is, "Be aware of the dynamic." If it's apparent that he'll just use the money to buy alcohol, give him an apple instead. As in wanting to effect social change, the real issues that arise about service are not in the context of extreme situations but in the day-to-day engagements we have with family, friends, co-workers, and those in our spiritual community.

Look at close relationships. These are the people we live with and say we love. Seeing them regularly, we have to be aware of their patterns and needs, and when something is being asked of us we must recognize where it's being asked from. We're conscious about responding, and where we respond from. This is what makes it real. It's not just about the action, but the awareness that underlies the action. Sometimes, not giving is the best way to serve. We have to be quiet and still enough to feel underneath what someone is asking, in order to really understand what we should do. Otherwise, our inability to step up might be just a reflection of our own limitation, cloaked as "discrimination."

The most important thing about service is not whether we respond to somebody else's need—it's whether we are prepared to respond. We have to look at ourselves instead of looking at whether their need is real or not real and then judging it. This always means penetrating through our misunderstanding and not theirs. If we respond to someone's need and they didn't need it, what do we lose? Only our contraction, our own inability to give. Service is about getting past our resistance to giving. This is how we grow, and ultimately, how we end up serving the highest in ourselves.

the most important thing about service is not whether we respond to somebody else's need—it's whether we are prepared to respond

We're always setting boundaries about how and when to serve. My personal experience is that we can be a lot bigger than we usually are, or feel that we can be. Breaking past our limited capacity to give is a major part of the real power of serving. If we feel, "I can't do more than this," and yet we do, it makes us bigger. By giving beyond our previous capacity to give we develop real internal muscle. As we stretch over time, what used to be a firm boundary is no longer there. In terms of physical fatigue, we may have to be conscious of how much we're doing, but the question is always, what depth are we conscious from? Look at someone like Mata Amritanandamayi (Amma), who gives *darśana* (darshan) for days on end, twelve to fourteen hours per session. How many

times does she leave while people are waiting, saying, "Sorry, I'm tired"? That just doesn't happen.

If we feel resistance coming up, we have to dig deeper, into a place that is never closed. If we're "serving" but are feeling grumpy about it, we may be helping out, but it's not really selfless service. The job may have gotten done, but we haven't changed inside. I've talked about the years I worked in the bakery. Some days it was not all that joyous and I was downright pissed off about being there—but the internal work I had to do to overcome those feelings was worth the effort. If we have to do something, shouldn't we benefit from the experience by growing? Service can never be dependent upon whether we feel like giving in that moment. In my own *sādhana*, the most expansive times were when I had to get past my unwillingness to serve, because there was some constraint in *me*, some limited ego, some "what about me?" in the equation. What I was concerned with was getting past that preoccupation with myself, because I wanted to serve a higher Self.

KNOW GOD BY SERVING HIM

I've said that whatever level of mastery I have achieved has happened from service, and that was expressed as service to God, guru, and community. Those are inseparable. I'm suggesting that if you truly want to know and love God, serve Him. If you don't know how to do that, then get quiet inside and ask, "How may I serve You?" It's a good question because we fear that if we offer ourselves to God we'll have to give up something important. But there's never a conflict between our life and living God's life, except if we misunderstand.

I lived in the ashram for thirty years and serving that community was not always easy. Yet I was grateful every day, because it gave me the opportunity to choose gratitude. I chose to come face-to-face with my inability to give. How else would I change? Other people traveled to exotic places with our teacher while I stayed home and worked. I found myself thinking, "Why do I have to do all this when nobody else has to?" I was the head teacher there, but I stayed behind and worked. In that sense, the situation was perfect. What was relevant was my reaction, what I chose to do, every time I felt contracted. In the end, I learned to rest in simplicity and do whatever was wanted.

We each have to ask ourselves: Do I want to know myself in my limited form or do I want to know myself as God? If we feel contraction it's a sign that we're reinforcing our limited understanding instead of seeking to know our highest Self. However, here's the catch: most likely, when we're asked to do something we don't want to do our first experience *is* going to be contraction. So we act. We understand we're in a struggle and we use the energy and power of will and action to penetrate through our limited knowledge. We can ask to understand why we're contracting around this, but instead of waiting around to get a clear answer, we simply serve. We're willing to reach through our own resistance to know the place underneath that resistance.

When we direct our powers of will, knowledge, and action toward liberation we free ourselves from bondage instead of reinforcing it. We free ourselves from self-serving will and from limited knowledge, and our actions are rooted in service. When our intention is to selflessly serve, we act in order to know God. As we create a flow with life by giving what is wanted, all our actions, even those that seem ordinary to others, are performed as a ritual of worship.

This is how we come to know the God within us who says, "Do with Me as you wish." How prepared are you to live in Śiva's mantra? If you want to be Śiva, to have His powers, then act like Him. Repeat this mantra in your own life: "Do with me as You wish." Then, have the commitment to act on that wish, no matter what resistance surfaces in you. In truth, our resistance is far more exhausting than any action we might perform. So stop feeling sorry for yourself and start giving. If your heart is closed, open it. Service is like a laser that cuts through all our bindings. When that happens, so many of the questions about service simply go away. We serve out of love, and from the gratitude for the possibility of knowing the God within us.

SERVING THE GODDESS APARA

As we learn to serve, even when we don't want to, we discover that in giving, we can either have the experience of resistance and struggle, or openness and joy. Our evolving experience is the result of our conscious choice, of knowing why we are engaging in seva. We get past "this is too hard," and all the other judgments we might have, because we are clear about what we want from life. We also come to recognize that we will have to pay to grow, and that payment is in the form of surrendering who we think we are and what we think we need.

We're really learning to serve Aparā, the goddess of action. We are growing by doing her will and living the mantra, "May all my actions serve You." (See Appendix B.) Unfortunately, our usual mantra is, "May *some* of my actions serve You." We pick and choose how, when, and in what circumstances we're willing to give. We bargain with Aparā, trying to substitute what we want to do for what is being asked of us. It is only by being willing to serve unconditionally that we truly ask to be transformed. We penetrate through our understanding of action and ask to know the higher purpose of every seemingly mundane thing we do.

When we're asked to serve or to give, who's really asking? Śiva, and His power of action, Aparā. So the next time somebody says, "Would you do the dishes?" know who's really making that request! More importantly, know who's responding when you say, "No." God asks, we say no. If you want to grow, give what is wanted, not what you want to give—and doing so will break your brain, it will break your bones, it will break your heart. True service will break everything in you that needs to be broken in order for you to recognize the perfection of giving.

When we understand the power of action and how we function within it, we also begin to see how attached we are to our bodies. Because so much of our experience centers around what's happening to us physically, we become very identified with our bodily form. We think, for example, that our body is moving from town to town rather than recognizing that our awareness is traveling. Service frees us from this focus on the physical. When you're too tired to continue working, it's ultimately not your body that continues to perform. It's really an exercise of your will, your own knowledge of why you're still working when your body is falling apart. Your life is not what you think it is. You are not your body. You *are* your *suṣumṇa*, an expression of eternal life, and the body is simply the grossest form of that energetic system.

SERVICE CONSUMES THE ENERGY OF THE MIND

So much of learning to serve involves the devouring of thought-constructs and consuming the energy of mind. This is important since our minds are continually seeking to define, and thought-constructs are simply the matrix of all those definitions of who we are and what we do. Consciousness thereby becomes encased in this web of thought-constructs and we engage in actions that spring forth from our needs, rather than acting for the purpose of self-knowledge.

Our actions must be in service to the goddess Parāpara for the purpose of gaining knowledge, not to produce an effect, or what is classically called "the fruit of action." We serve because we want to know ourselves, not because we want to get something or are looking for any result. We simply ask, "May I know You as my Self," so that we may share God's knowledge of who He is. Then we act and extend that awareness into our lives. We seek to do what is asked of us, and offer what is needed—and that is the essence of unconditional, selfless service.

All of our actions, if in service to God, are breaking down our basic misunderstanding about who we're actually serving. We think we are serving someone different than ourself, but we are really opening to the higher knowledge that we're not only serving God, but that we *are* God. Service breaks down dualistic thinking and teaches us that there is only one Consciousnes, expressing itself as diversity, and interacting within itself. We learn that through us, God is serving Himself in the form of others. This is the meaning of, "May I know You as my Self." By changing how and why we act, we start living from a higher consciousness, and we know who we're serving. We don't need to hear the applause.

It is only by devouring our thought-constructs that we free ourselves from the trap of, "I want something and I'll only do this if I get it." As we repeat the mantra, "May I know You as my Self, may I give what is wanted," we are penetrating through our self-centered patterns, creating an inner resonance that will transform our experience. We must consciously choose to do this. Nobody makes us do it, except our teacher! The most compassionate thing a teacher does is free us from ourselves. That includes breaking down our unwillingness to serve and our attachment to getting something from serving.

all of our actions, if in service to god, are breaking down our basic misunderstanding about who we're actually serving

Quite often, those in a spiritual practice will serve the teacher directly, and other issues tend to arise in this dynamic. We may serve because of our need to prove ourselves worthy (my teacher will love me if I do this) or due to our insecurity (my teacher will not love me if I don't do this). A teacher must therefore free us from fear and from self-rejection, which are key elements in such motivations. Whenever these feelings are in the equation it's not really service but some form of manipulation. We think we know what we'll get out of such "service," or what we'll avoid because of it. We end up acting from a place of constriction or resentment, not from an open heart. These are all limitations that make service conditional, and therefore not true seva.

When you recognize that you serve out of tension, resistance, fear, or self-rejection, you must be willing to burn that level of functioning. This sutra says, "Service is the charnel ground, ablaze with the fire of Consciousness." Understand that if you offer yourself into that fire, you have to remain there long enough for the blaze to incinerate you! When I see a student grumbling about the work I've given, I just give them some more; I throw another log on the fire. This is the only way I can help students burn through the limited capacity to give. All resistance is a fight against being willing to give, without thought of price. When we truly surrender to serving the Divine, we are simply immersed in God's love and witness its expression, flowing out from us to wherever it is needed.

Sādhana is your own charnel ground, and seva produces the hottest fire. In it, you discover that growing is not about you.

Not only do we sacrifice the demands of our small self, but we come to know that being free is not a personal experience: it is the freeing *from* the personal. The dissolution of thought-construct is critical in gaining liberation because the mind is the functioning capacity that sustains the awareness of separateness. Thought-construct perpetuates our attachment to objects—to anything we perceive as outside ourself, including the people and dynamics in our lives.

We want to free ourselves from the mind, which can only give us the dualistic experience of "myself" and "everything other than myself" (i.e., objects). It's a limited form of knowledge. Pure knowledge is: "I am all things. All this is me." We ourselves create objects and then have to dissolve our attachment to them. When we engage those objects from the mind, we're stuck, because the mind can *only* attach. If we engage from our heart, from a place that knows "I am all these things," then there's no attachment. Everything is part of us, and we're not seeking to attract or hold anything in order to complete ourselves.

STILLNESS OF THOUGHT

The Spandakārikās describe the pulsating of creation as an arising and subsiding. This important Tantric text is believed to have been written by the sage Vasugupta (circa 860–925) as a commentary on the Śiva Sutras. A significant aspect of this practice is not attaching energy and form to thought. As a thought arises, it's like a wave on the ocean. If you're walking along the beach and a beautiful wave arises, you don't think, "That's the one! There can never be another wave like that one." It just dissolves on the beach without our grabbing and holding on to it. The mind wants to do the opposite, to define and hold on to whatever we encounter. So the devouring of thought-construct frees us from the mind's tendency to attach to an object, thereby creating happiness or unhappiness.

The Spandakārikās describe the essential problem: "The arising of mental representation marks the disappearance of the flavor of the supreme nectar of immortality. Due to this, man forfeits his freedom." A statement like this, written by a great saint, is giving us a simple message: Stop believing your mind. Stop defining your experience by living in your mind. Throw your thoughts into the fire of Consciousness. This is absolutely a prerequisite to freeing yourself from limited identity because the matrix of your thought-constructs is the very center of your identity. It creates a weave of experience centered around your belief that you are a separate individual, and the mind perpetually reinforces that experience of separation.

This is what all great saints have told us, and it is why we seek higher knowledge. As soon as we begin to detach from our thoughts, we get a glimpse that our identity (out of which all those thoughts emerge) has been a limited one. Then, we can start to let go of that limited identity. Rudi, with his focus on energy and flow, was really emphasizing the necessity of dissolving all thought, all resistance, all inability to give. All of these limitations come from the grasping belief, "I am *this* and I must have *that* in

the highest service is simply offering our will into shiva's will

order to be who I am." Rudi taught us to take the energy from our mind and put it into the flow within our psychic mechanism. Once we are established in that internal energy, we extend the flow from our center outward, engaging what's required of us in life from that place.

This is how we serve and how we dissolve thought-construct. Instead of projecting our demands and dumping our tensions on others, we open our heart and feel the flow with them. There's an interchange of energy and openness rather than the opposite, which only contracts everyone involved. What greater service can you imagine than to simply live in flow with the people around you? Why not be simple and open without demanding that others behave as you require? Only thoughts close the heart.

We've seen that the highest service is offering our will into Śiva's will. In the abstract, that may seem like a great idea, but when our resistance to change surfaces, we become willful. This is why we must unconditionally serve Parā, the energy and power of Śiva's supreme will. That is how we merge our own awareness into the highest consciousness. We recognize our true nature, unobstructed by thought-construct—like seeing ourselves in a perfect mirror—and we witness all of life as the outpouring of that supreme awareness. This is not accomplished by individual effort, but by the innate expression of Śiva's freedom, pulling us back home.

God's will is the experience of freedom. Our will, expressed in everything we do, is really about us trying to get something, which just perpetuates our suffering. Seems like a clear choice, doesn't it? But the trick is that we have to *give up* our own will, which keeps trying to reassert itself. We think, "I don't want to serve anymore . . . I'm too tired . . . why does my teacher make me do this?" These thought-constructs are all part of what we must burn.

Instead of griping about giving up your own will, follow Parā's lead. Surrender to her and open to God's will. Then there's only God asking you to do something—and how are you going to deny that which gave you life? Isn't it amazing that most people harbor a deep unwillingness to serve the God they claim to love and want to know. In our minds we insist, "*That's* not the highest service, I know better than that," or, "I can do this, but I won't do that." These are the ways we define and limit what we're willing to give.

If you ask, "May my will be Your will," you must be willing to live through the request, to have pressed in your face how much you function from your own will. So do not repeat this mantra unless you mean it—and then it's never, ever, about what somebody else asked you to do, only what you're asking yourself to do. Understand that you will meet your resistance and you will rail against it. One moment you might be in the bliss of surrender, with tears of joy flowing out of your heart, and the next moment the tears express, "My God, I can't take it—and I won't." Both reactions are real. In fact, you repeat the mantra consciously so that the resistance *does* arise. Our self-reflective capacity of consciousness enables us to know we function from a limited place and still affirm, "I wish to grow." This is a conscious effort, just as it is Śiva's active effort to express freedom. We are asking to live in the energy of will exerted by Consciousness itself. The fire of Consciousness has done its work only when individual will is completely surrendered to God's will.

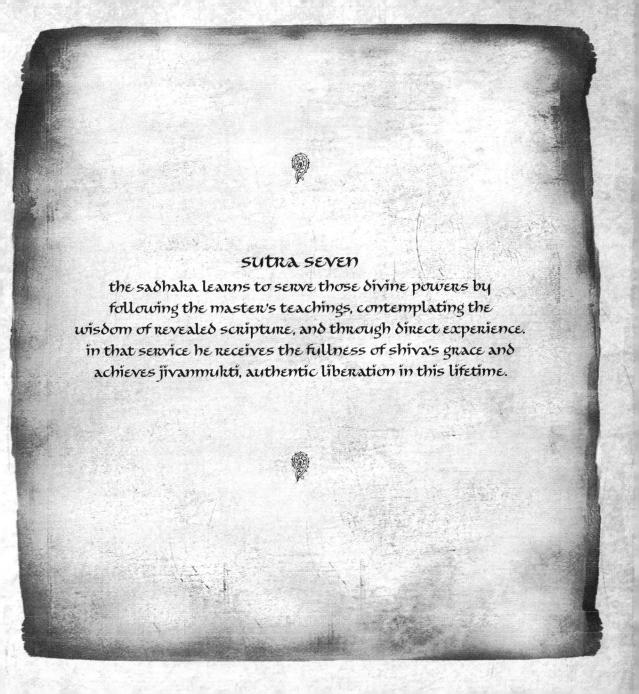

SUTRA SEVEN

the sadhaka learns to serve those divine powers by
following the master's teachings, contemplating the
wisdom of revealed scripture, and through direct experience.
in that service he receives the fullness of shiva's grace and
achieves jivanmukti, authentic liberation in this lifetime.

A relationship with a teacher, studying scripture, and doing our own practices are all elements in gaining access to the divine powers of will, knowledge, and action. Through the grace of that contact and our unwavering devotion to God, we begin to really understand those powers and create shifts in our awareness. What we learn from a teacher or read in scripture is important, but it must be confirmed in our own experience. That's what makes it *our* truth, instead of someone else's truth. All authentic teachings emphasize that we discover our Self through our own consciousness and the power of our reflective capacity to know our state. This is the only place we can truly have this experience and merge with God. Our internal practice, the discipline of our *sādhana*, is the foundation for engaging with life in order to understand its truth.

The problem with relying on direct experience, however, is that we continually look through our own lens, based on what has happened in the past. Everything we think and know is filtered through a limited perspective that keeps trying to find God in something "other." Even our own spiritual practice is often caught in the duality of, "I am meditating, I am doing seva, I am doing this in order to know that I am God." That's fine, since we have to start where we are. But we have to reach past our programming, which is mired in dualistic thinking, and that's hard to do because we can't see outside our mental box. The *upāyas* (which we'll discuss in detail in Sutra Ten) describe the means of spiritual practice—how we as individuals come to directly know, "I am Śiva"—through the path of effort, the path of energy and the dissolution of thought-construct, and the path of awareness. Another way of describing the *upāyas* would be to say that they offer various means to penetrate through our own experience, to reveal an unlimited perspective.

The Sanskrit term *vāsanā* means "impression," the residue of past experience that is in the mind, in our consciousness. We function through these impressions, which reinforce the vision of duality that insists that there's *me* and there's *this* and *that*, instead of seeing unity. Meditation is tuning in to God. We can have a mind filled with turmoil and yet we're able to sit down and find the divine inside. The direct experience we're looking for in meditation comes from having the discipline to penetrate through the noise that arises from all those *vāsanās*. We need that discipline to work through our monkey mind, to sit down and reach past our crazy thoughts, past all the obsessions that grip our attention. All of that commotion stems from the impressions that have been left in us as we engage life.

meditation is tuning in to god

This is not to say that we should be aloof from daily living. Quite the contrary. But the purpose of that engagement should be to gain knowledge, to raise our level of awareness above our past experience. Impressions are like the clouds that block the sun so completely that we forget it was once there. Much of the power of the direct experience gained in meditation is therefore not only in the contact—in getting very quiet and being one with God—but in the new impression that's left when we open our eyes and engage what appears to be a field of diversity that's separate from God. We've made contact with that stillness inside and have created a different resonance from which to function—one that can penetrate through all outward experience and discover the same unity everywhere.

Although the key to having a deeper direct experience is making contact with oneness, you may find that it's sometimes harder to reach that place of stillness. It might be that you're expecting to repeat a specific experience and this prevents you from turning inside. But on other days, something else might be happening: the fire that you've created in yourself will dislodge some deeper tension or pattern, and that appears as surface noise. As those latent impressions are revealed, a myriad of thoughts start dancing. If this occurs, don't get caught in the content of these thoughts, but understand that what's been released is actually condensed energy. This is a good thing. It informs us that we have to apply more discipline to consume all that energy and to put it into flow. Deal with it from that perspective instead of berating yourself for not being "good enough" to hold on to quietness.

So much of the time our own experience is not of God, not of unity, but of duality. We don't consciously think, "Oh dear, today I'm having a dualistic experience," but we feel the effects of that duality in our tensions and patterns. The problem is then compounded, because when we're fighting with life and beating the hell out of ourselves or others, we end up reinforcing the same level of consciousness that we've been functioning from—the underlying resonance that's creating our painful experience. If you're a tense person your experience of life will be one of tension. How could it be otherwise?

THE POWER OF SHAKTIPAT

The purpose of having a teacher or reading scripture is to point us to a different experience. Particularly in a relationship with a teacher who embodies a living spiritual force, this means more than just pointing the way. Through the power of *śaktipāta*, the teacher creates a pathway within us that leads to a higher experience and provides us with the energy to travel on that road. *Śaktipāta* is an energetic transmission, a laser beam that cuts through the density of our experience of duality, our mind, and every instrument playing in the accompanying orchestra. This transmission projects a higher force, a bigger, stronger energy that creates an internal resonance we can feel and attune to.

the purpose of having a teacher or reading scripture is to point us to a different experience

That resonance is already within us, but for most people, it needs to be activated in order to be directly experienced. It requires a teacher to pierce through our mind and emotions so that we open to what is present inside us. From the perspective of the student, *śaktipāta* is usually felt as coming at or being delivered to them. And that's true when experienced in the duality of "there's me and there's the teacher." In the field of Śiva's heart, however, there is no inside or outside to any experience. So it's never that something is being put in you, but rather that an energy field is set up that activates what is already there.

Śaktipāta is the descent of grace and it arouses *kuṇḍalinī*. There are a few individuals who didn't need a teacher for grace to have penetrated into them. Someone like Nityananda evokes a deep response in us because we recognize the power in such a rare person. Others, like Rudi, worked for years and years to create enough openness to feel and absorb grace. Rudi described himself as being like a wild ox who was continually turning around a grindstone, wearing down his density and resistance. It was grace itself that gave him the energy and the insight to yoke himself to this arduous work. It was strenuous, required discipline, and most of the time it wasn't easy. This is the same grace that manifested in Nityananda with apparent effortlessness.

I would say that the relationship with a teacher who gives *śaktipāta* is the highest grace. We're really in a relationship with the energy itself, a force that has the capacity to cut through every level of density and misunderstanding. Even when we resist, *śaktipāta* is not responding to us, but to the very grace that called that energy to itself. What does this tell us? Get out of the way! Once that energy is activated it awakens itself and it's going to call forth to itself that which it needs—which of course is itself. All resistance is futile. However Śiva's grace descends into us, our responsibility is to respond to the wish to grow, which grace itself planted in us.

My own *sādhana* began when I met Rudi. I sat in my first class and for the next forty-five minutes I saw nothing but the whites of his eyes. Everything else disappeared and my heart exploded. That was my introduction to *śaktipāta*. Rudi provided a direct, powerful transmission of grace, but it required a lifetime of work to open to the full potential of that experience. I spent years focused on absorbing the energy of *śaktipāta* and didn't begin reading scripture until much later. I found that the ancient texts then confirmed what I had already discovered in myself.

When this activation happens at a young age, as it did for me, we aren't usually mature enough to recognize that Śiva is trying to free us. The deepest part of us has called that freedom forth, and that's when and why we receive *śaktipāta*. We come in contact with an energy field that's bigger than us, strong enough to penetrate through our own level of unconsciousness. Looking back at my life and recognizing the degree of density that I functioned from in my youth, it amazes me that I could have attracted such grace. So I have always felt very grateful, and my experience established in me the permanent awareness that God was entering my life even though I hadn't formally invited Him in. Why is not important. The only thing that's been important to me is my response to grace.

THE TEACHER CUTS THROUGH OUR TENSIONS

As Rudi's student there was one challenge: Could you open your heart big enough to absorb the tidal wave of energy that was coming at you? A matchbox-sized heart could not possibly take it all in. In Rudi's presence your life was palpably changing due to the sheer power of the grace. He threw energy around like a hundred-armed Śiva. Rudi understood that it had nothing to do with him—he was just the instrument through which *śaktipāta* flowed—yet he understood the responsibility inherent in being that conduit.

There were two sides to Rudi: his unconditional love, and the laser sword that obliterated your smallness if he saw you either not opening or starting to close. I think of him as the fastest samurai sword in the West. Before you even knew what hit you, he would slice through your tension, which felt like he was cutting *you* in two! My experience of this, however, was that as soon as my lopped-off head started falling to the ground, Rudi was holding me. His basic premise was that if you were sitting with him, you wanted to be open. Anything else that was happening, any resistance that showed up in the process, was something for him to cut through.

freeing someone from themselves is perhaps the highest expression of love and compassion

Rudi didn't need to be nice or be concerned with your feelings. He simply recognized and respected the power of transmission so much that he would not allow you to close, even for a moment. He gave you the energy to do the work, and if you didn't, he either sliced and diced you or threw you out! But I never, ever felt that he was doing anything other than helping me to grow. Now that I'm in the role of the teacher, I appreciate Rudi from the perspective of knowing that freeing someone from themselves is perhaps the highest expression of love and compassion.

In contrast to Rudi, Nityananda mostly sat in silence. Yet in his presence, people had much the same experience of being opened and changed. This is the grace of *śaktipāta*. What do we care what it feels like, or what needs to be rearranged within us to create freedom? Working with a teacher can be intense because the sheer power of *śaktipāta* is being unleashed through that relationship. However, it's never the person of the teacher who frees us, but grace itself in the form of energy.

Any authentic teacher will recognize that he or she is simply allowing that grace to flow through them, as it chooses. That grace is the power of Śiva Himself, creating an opening in us, providing the means for us to turn our awareness inside, and giving us the capacity to know Him as our Self.

Your relationship with a teacher is not different from your relationship with your wish to grow and to know God. When it's hard and your resistance is showing up, would you stop and say, "Forget it God, I've changed my mind"? It is due to your capacity to live in clarity and commitment that you can receive the highest grace from a teacher, through *śaktipāta*. Eventually, it is only your own state of complete surrender that brings you to the moment where you no longer need a teacher. If you engage with a teacher for any other purpose than to have your ego dissolved, to help you free yourself from dualistic thinking, you're engaging for the wrong reason. Don't have anyone for a teacher who doesn't love you enough to free you from your ego.

THE TEACHER-STUDENT RELATIONSHIP

The single purpose of our relationship with a teacher is to be supported in establishing our direct experience of unity with God. If you are clear that liberation is the most important thing in your life, then ask this question when considering having a teacher: Will I achieve my freedom without this relationship? Once we recognize the need for guidance, there may be other questions to ask about a particular teacher: Who is this person serving? Are they serving themselves or serving me so that I may have my own connection with God? It is only in stillness, in your self-reflective capacity of consciousness, that you can honestly answer these questions.

It's important not to judge a teacher from your ego but from a deep awareness of what you really want from that relationship. Especially when you've been given an answer or some instruction that was not what you wanted to hear, remember why you engaged the teacher in the first place. Make sure you're following the teachings, even when you don't agree with them. Surrender to the teacher—not as a person, but to the energy and consciousness that flows through them to you. Surrender is always an internal work that breaks down our resistance to being changed.

the single purpose of our relationship with a teacher is to be supported in establishing our direct experience of unity with god

Abhinavagupta's beautiful description of the teacher-student relationship is the most powerful articulation of the subject that I have ever encountered:

> *Ultimately, entering into a relationship with a teacher is the conscious choice on the part of the student to place his*

finite awareness in direct confrontation with the expanded consciousness of the teacher, which is the unbounded consciousness the student wishes to attain. This meeting of finite and infinite consciousness represents the very condition of vimarśa, Consciousness doubling back on itself, the method of realization that abides perpetually in and as the divine heart. As the student comes into the gaze of the guru, his finite consciousness encounters its own source in the person of the teacher. It releases the inner meditative current, the liberating grace, the self-referential nature of the unbounded Consciousness of Śiva. In the process, the teacher binds the student to service and growth and the inner practices required. The single purpose of the binding is the attainment of freedom. The teacher acts as God's agent to free the student from himself. This all happens through śaktipāta, the will of Śiva that has taken the disciple into the gaze of the guru.

Do not engage a teacher in a *śaktipāta* lineage if you don't want your life to change! If you have engaged a teacher, remember to pay attention to the part of you that asked to be a student—not to the part of you that is unwilling to change. Listening to, and from, this deepest place enables us to respond to grace. From the moment we first felt grace, and in every moment after that initial contact, our responsibility is to let go, open, and recognize that Parā is emerging from within. She is being awakened as the power of *kuṇḍalinī*, calling forth to herself the energy she needs to arise, as well as the consciousness needed to create the dynamics of life that forge that awakening as our permanent experience.

In the Tantrāloka, Abhinavagupta said that a *sādhaka* should have either a yogi as a teacher or a *jñāni* (a person of knowledge) and that the lucky student has one who is both. My own focus has been that of a yogi, but I have a great appreciation for scripture. At its highest, scripture is considered to be revealed by Śiva, through the agency of saints. Scripture is another form of *śaktipāta*, the transmission of energy through word. The power of scripture is the resonance that it functions in. Scripture resonates with *buddhi*, the level of consciousness that has the capacity for discernment. *Buddhi* is above mind, above thought. When it hears scripture, it recognizes: This is the truth. Pay attention to scripture from that level instead of trying to analyze it from your mind.

As we listen to or read scripture, we tune in to the truth. It's like what often happens through poetry: our heart simply opens. Scripture creates a level of resonance in us that the mind is not capable of reaching on its own. It may just be one word or phrase that clicks, that creates an internal "ping" of that truth, but that is enough to shift us out of our perspective, Of course, whatever we learn from scripture or from a teacher must be confirmed and made real in our own daily life. Otherwise, it's only someone else's experience.

The activity of daily life should open us to the experience of unity instead of continuing to reinforce our experience of duality. Living in unity means freedom from personal identity, from any experience of being separate from or different than God. This is *jīvanmukti*, liberation while alive. Rarely do people come into a spiritual practice thinking, "I want to be liberated, I want to know that I am Śiva." Mostly, we just want to alleviate suffering, but what we don't initially understand is that all suffering is due to our perceived separation from Śiva.

Did you know that every country-western song is really about being separate from Śiva? That fundamental suffering is interpreted as, "My lover did me wrong," or, "I'll die because I don't have a lover, or enough money." The mind takes our underlying sense of incompleteness and finds specific reasons for our unhappiness, in a dimension of consciousness that can only perceive on its own level. Make no mistake: the mind, as a tool of the ego, does that in order to sustain itself and its own experience, and too often, we buy into that sad song.

Texts in every religion depict the battle between your small self and the part of you that knows it's God. And guess what? This is a battle that you, as an individual, will eventually lose. Our relationship with grace is for the sole purpose of guiding us to that moment and giving us the strength and clarity to surrender ourselves. To get there, we must penetrate through every level of perception of ourself as a limited, separate identity, including the belief that we exist only because we have a body.

In our *sādhana* we are trying to merge our individuated experience—past even experiencing God within ourself—into one of God experiencing through us and as us. *Jīvanmukti* means being liberated from any impression of separateness. There's no longer a sense of going between the experience of separateness and unity. Ultimately, you recognize that God is not even freeing *you*, but simply experiencing His freedom in every dimension of life, through you. Don't do spiritual practice if you think it's for any other reason than unconditional surrender to God. You may not have known this coming in to your practice, but now you do. And here's the kicker: You will never be there to experience your liberation. The ego never gets enlightened.

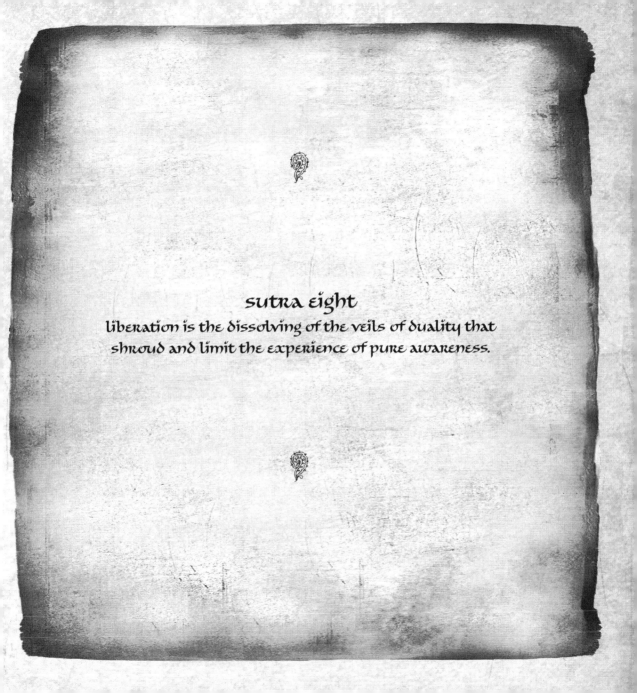

sutra eight
liberation is the dissolving of the veils of duality that
shroud and limit the experience of pure awareness.

Duality is a single experience that can be seen as having two aspects, external and internal. The apparent, external duality is the life we see before us every day. We walk on the earth, there are people, trees, and animals, and we live in the misunderstanding that all of that is not part of the whole. Our *sādhana* transforms our experience of diversity to the point that we directly perceive that the world and all the objects in it are not separate or different from Śiva—and He is none other than our Self. When we see and engage our world as objects we miss the fact that everything is actually just energy: cosmic force condensing into form. It's understandable to think, "There's me and there's the tree and we're separate," but we're really only diverse expressions of the same divine powers.

We find many challenges in the world, particularly in our interactions with the "objects" that look like other people. We don't have a problem watching a mango tree going through its cycles, bearing fruit. It's in the realm of human interaction that we struggle. This is an aspect of duality we must live in and penetrate through in order to understand that this part of the expressed world is also simply energy and perfect in its form. In the midst of our engagement with people, perhaps due to feeling some pain or suffering, we have a tremendous need for others to be different, to conform to how we think they should be. We continually attempt to create our idea of perfection, and as we get caught in that struggle, we lose ourselves and suffer.

It's natural that this happens, and it is why we must get very quiet and still inside—to really look at our interaction to understand what's happening, instead of unconsciously interacting. It is in our experience of all this worldly duality that we transcend the appearance of separation. This is a fundamental canon of Tantric practice, and something that distinguishes it from many other practices, which will advise you to leave the world. Your daily life will prove to be the cremation ground of all your misunderstanding. So we engage and open to the world, create a flow with it, and understand it as energy that is projecting from our own consciousness.

our experience is always based on our level of awareness

Our experience is always based on our level of awareness. We are constantly creating some drama and performing as the leading actor in the stage production, and only we determine if it's a sad or joyful story. As we engage with life, it's always our choice to continue the fight or penetrate through whatever is happening to see the unity in all the diversity. One of the simplest ways the *upāyas* describe the progression of freedom in Tantric practice is that it's a transition from living in diversity (in duality), to seeing the unity in all that diversity, to experiencing just unity. None are in conflict with the other, but these different levels of experience are based on where we live in ourselves, where our consciousness is focused.

EXTERNAL AND INTERNAL DUALITY

If we want the highest experience, we must develop the capacity to perceive unity. Otherwise, if we say, "I just want to live in unity," we are essentially rejecting our life and creating duality in our thinking. We're stating: I want to live *there*, but not *here*. I can only be happy if I live *there* instead of *here*. We've immediately separated "there" and "here." This demonstrates the incredible power of our minds, which reinforce separation by continually engaging diversity from thought-constructs that can only perceive in terms of duality.

An important aspect of our *sādhana* is the dissolving of dualistic thought. This work is critical, because so much of our interaction in life is affected by what I call "the grip of the ego." This is the fight we are constantly embroiled in as the result of functioning from misunderstanding, from duality. Our work is to free ourselves from that grip—from our needs, fears, and demands. Those tensions are always a reflection of a more limited awareness. It's only when we develop an expanded awareness in ourselves that we can engage the very same life that caused us to struggle, and create openness instead of suffering. One click of the dial determines what we tune in to: understanding, joy, and openness, or tension, fighting, and closing.

External duality refers to something we experience as outside ourselves. But although there is the sense that "we" are fighting with "it," we're really just duking it out with ourselves, and therefore need to consider what can be called *internal* duality.

This is the real place of bondage, the experience we must cut through to find our liberation. It is within our own awareness that we encounter the veils of duality that cloud our ability to know "I am God. I am the light, and all this is me."

Liberation means union with God. It is the experience of the simple, unconditional joy of our own existence, that arises when we penetrate through the veils. Unfortunately, all the fight we have with apparent external duality obfuscates what is important in life. We lose track not only of what we really want to do, but of the true source of suffering. We don't understand what is actually keeping us enmeshed in separation because we're constantly looking for external causes of our suffering. The reasons we come up with are endless: My mommy and daddy didn't love me when I was young, this person doesn't love me now, I don't have the ideal job or some particular thing in my life.

liberation means union with god. it is the experience of the simple, unconditional joy of our own existence.

THE REAL SOURCE OF OUR PAIN

The truth is that we *do* suffer for all those reasons, but if we look deeper, we see that suffering is a pointer. When we think, "I don't have what I want. I don't have what I need. I don't have what I think fulfills me," it is our mental constructs that cause us to contract inside, and this is what creates suffering. The problem perpetuates itself because, when we are confused—believing that we suffer when we do or don't have something—we immediately try to change these conditions. We move on to thinking: If I just get a partner I'm going to be happy, or if I get rid of my partner, or if I didn't have to work. It's always some "thing" or another. We're constantly trying to do something, get something, or change something.

Although Tantric practices emphasize that we must consume and celebrate the world, we must learn, from that interaction, that the world will never completely satisfy. The problem is that although, on some level, we already know this, we don't really absorb the lesson because we're so busy reaching and doing, again and again. We're easily seduced by the idea that some next thing will bring us ultimate fulfillment.

Due to all this aggravation, we end up in a constant fight on the mental and emotional levels. We forget that the sense of emptiness is the real source of our pain and suffering. No matter how many things we get, happiness simply doesn't last because we're taking the wrong medicine for the wrong ailment. We just aren't prepared to suspend the belief that *we need something* in order to be whole. The reality is that we need nothing; we only need to recognize that wholeness exists within us, perfect at every moment. This flips the search for fulfillment on its head. We're no longer seeking to find something outside of ourselves, something separate or different from us, in order to experience joy and wholeness. We're only discovering what's already present within each of us.

the reality is that we need nothing; we only need to recognize that wholeness exists within us, perfect at every moment

The cause of our suffering is not what we think it is, and moreover, it's not what we perpetually reinforce that it is. And as soon as we begin to look for the true cause of suffering, two things happen. First, we start to realize that this *thing* isn't the cause of our suffering (and if it is, it's only because we're choosing to suffer in that dimension). Second, we get still enough to experience the very real veils of separation in us. Understand that this is not the superficial pain of feeling separation between you and the person you want to be with. The pain of being separate from God is the true cause of suffering—and it definitely hurts!

Although we may theoretically understand these ideas, there is often a gap between what we know and our direct experience. That's why we do *sādhana*. There is a transition in our experience, and the various practices we do are the means to implement this progressive change. At the highest level is the state of pure awareness in which all fulfillment resides, but most of us don't initially find ourselves there. What isn't entirely self-evident to people is that the key to having that experience is to look for it. This doesn't mean we deny the experience we're having, but if we focus on not being "there," we don't look to find and experience the veils of duality and dissolve them. We keep looking within this "I'm not there yet" experience and keep reinforcing the same dynamic.

FOCUSING ON WHAT WE REALLY WANT

Whenever my eldest brother leaves me, he says, "Keep your eye on Jesus." That's another way of saying that we have to pay attention to our inner state while engaging in the world. Otherwise, we keep looking for joy in places that it doesn't exist or can't sustain itself and we thereby reinforce separation, the true source of our pain. So we must find simplicity and joyfulness within, and then extend outward from there. Then, everything we do is infused with the same wholeness we found in ourselves. This is what Rudi called being established in both vertical and horizontal flow.

All action should be for the purpose of learning to engage life unconditionally. We begin to experience: I am Śiva, I am all things, and it is perfect. Even our spouse or partner is a perfect expression of that truth. And it isn't that *they're* perfect, but that our understanding is perfect. All relationships, and every interaction with the world, will either free you or bind you. That's why you must engage life with consciousness, employing your self-reflective capacity to free yourself of your attachment to how you think the world should be.

all action is for the purpose of learning how to engage the world unconditionally

As we free ourselves from our attachment to the world, we're also freeing ourselves from any attachment to our own separate identity. Both are necessary. Being free from the duality of the world is a prerequisite to liberation. It is only when we're no longer in the grip of horizontal dualistic experience that we can free ourselves from vertical dualistic experience.

Look again at the *tattva* chart. It shows the vertical descending and ascending of Consciousness. That verticality is the pathway to liberation. The chart shows how supreme Consciousness descends into form, and then, apparent duality is created. As that appearance of duality is consumed back into Consciousness and rises into what is understood and experienced as pure awareness, none of that form remains. There is no expressed duality for us to get confused about. Everything is experienced as Śiva, as our Self.

This may sound like a philosophical description, but the transformation of our consciousness happens within our psychic body. We use the three powers of will, knowledge, and action not only to create our experience of life in the world, but to work internally to bring our awareness and energy up through the *suṣumṇa*. Everything exists in the *suṣumṇa*. All levels of misunderstanding and unconsciousness as well as Consciousness itself reside there. The *suṣumṇa* serves as the refinery of the density of our consciousness, freeing it from any boundary, removing all darkness, and allowing our individual awareness to merge back into its source.

Every dimension of our consciousness—our mind, emotions, senses, as well as our deepest consciousness—is all fueled, engaged, and informed by our awareness. Higher consciousness is not like an uplifting quote we stick on a board. It's an experience we're looking for, and it requires that we keep penetrating through whatever is getting in the way of having that experience. That's the point: we have to penetrate through the veils of duality, which are so thin you can't see them. I often describe them as being like the material surgical gloves are made of. If you push against it, the membrane keeps stretching thinner and thinner, until finally the built-up pressure springs you backward. We can only penetrate through the veils of duality when we stop pushing and struggling long enough to let God pull us home.

as we free ourselves from our attachment to the world, we're also freeing ourselves from any attachment to our own separate identity

It's said that God is finer than the finest and subtler than the subtlest. So look for God and liberation in that which you cannot see instead of in what you do see. Look inside. You'll find not only the veils, but the unity on the other side of them. When we talk about internal and external duality, we're really just discussing one thing. Although we have to penetrate through our current experience from both directions, it's easier to start by reaching inside.

Nityananda advises that one must find the fastest and most effective means to get back home. So we start in meditation: focusing our awareness, repeatedly penetrating through our limited experience of consciousness. Once we've made contact with the resonance of unity we can radiate back out, shine a light on whatever we're looking at, and learn to serve from that state of openness. We can't help but see life completely differently. We can't find unity in the heart and not experience and express it in the world.

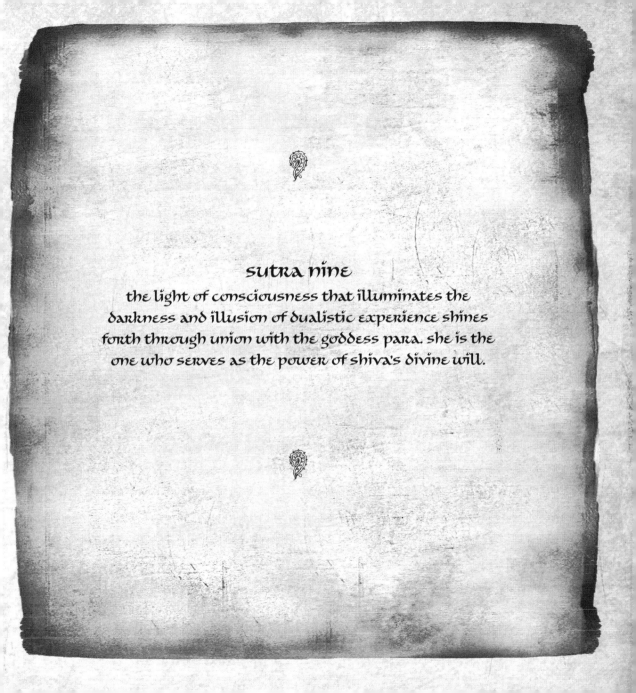

sutra nine

the light of consciousness that illuminates the
darkness and illusion of dualistic experience shines
forth through union with the goddess para. she is the
one who serves as the power of shiva's divine will.

As we repeat the mantras in the guided meditations, we tune in to that resonance of offering ourselves. The goddess Parā is the power of Śiva's will—the very power through which Śiva manifested Himself as the universe. We're asking the force of that energy and awareness to subtly, yet powerfully, shift our resonance away from the contraction we function in so much of the time. This shift allows us to palpably feel something deeper and finer inside. You could say that our role is to serve the one who serves the One.

This use of mantra is one form of meditation. Whenever we close our eyes we're attempting to come in contact with a deeper energy, a deeper awareness, beyond what we normally experience as "me." That's how we learn to experience ourselves not as our limited identity but as a bigger awareness that's not bound by the perception of duality or separation. We achieve freedom through our will, through our wish, penetrating back through what Abhinavagupta called "Śiva's powers of emission" to the source of all manifestation. All this resides within us.

By consuming Śiva's powers of will, knowledge, and action we live through and experience those very same powers as our own. In the process, we're consuming our limited understanding and experience of those energies, becoming one with these powers of Śiva's emission. This is not an abstract idea. It is how we can transform *our* experience. Every action, every thought, everything we think we know, our attempts to reach and get something—these are all expressions of the three powers. We function from and through them, using those energies to either reinforce our limited experience of them or to transform it.

POINTING OUR GPS

Our powers are not different or separate from Śiva's pure powers of awareness. They are simply the same powers, manifest in us, and as us. Our *sādhana* is to fine-tune our capacity to be aware so that we recognize the resonance of those powers. We come to know when we're caught in a limited perspective versus when we're surrendering that limitation. Only then can we see that we are those same energies and we can live from and function from a higher awareness. Just like penetrating through the veils of duality, so much depends on what address we program into our GPS (God's Positioning System). Where are *you* wanting to go?

Through the grace of Parā we hear God calling. Parā is also inclusive of Parāparā and Aparā, so if we really want to know the truth of life, we must start with our will. We point our will, our wish, in the direction of freedom—toward the bliss of the simplicity of our own existence—and then everything we want to know and do falls into place. Our will is like the engine of a train. The other powers follow that driving force because they are never separate from each other, just as they are never separate from their source.

Parā is also the power of Śiva's grace. The Muslims simply say, "*Inshallah*"—"if God wills it." The problem is that when we say that, we immediately start getting caught up in the mundane level of what that means. We end up asking, "Is getting a new home God's will or is it my will?" We forget that Śiva is only expressing one thing through His power of will: the expansion of His own experience of joy and freedom. That is His single focus. Whether we get a new home or not is irrelevant. What *is* relevant is whether our heart is open. God only uses His will to exclaim, "Let there be light. Let there be joy."

Using a mantra focuses our power of choice. By asking, "May my will be Your will. May I know You as my Self," we are deeply centering ourselves and directing our awareness. We're activating our wish to know and love God. From Śiva's perspective, we are never *not* in union with Him, but we do get lost in the emission of God's powers and therefore have to bring our attention out of the manifest world, back to the source of our existence.

the use of mantra focuses our power of choice

Our experience is that we mostly just act. We end up running into walls, mowing over people, doing everything in a state that's essentially unconscious. Aparā, the goddess of action, is typically shown looking rather like Kālī. She is red, has fangs, holds a few skulls, and her tongue is sticking out! Aparā is depicted that way to demonstrate the devouring power of action, a power that leads us to being lost in the grossest form of duality.

We have to look for the true purpose of action, which is to know ourselves. All the powers that create manifestation come from one unmanifest source and it is only when Śiva's powers move into action that the infinite begins to have form. So we have to work back through the power of action to discover the source of action. This reconnection is critical because without it, our wish to be free will not always get expressed in what we actually do. Even though we have the power to create the life we choose, we don't use our will to act in freedom or even with the goal of attaining liberation foremost in our sight. It is only when we are centered, expressing the higher consciousness we find in ourselves, that we create and reinforce freedom. Otherwise, we remain bound by our unconscious actions.

we have to look for the true purpose of action, which is to know ourselves

WILLFULNESS LIMITS US

The power of divine will wishes for one thing: to express the freedom of God's own Consciousness, the state of autonomous, unconditional bliss and joy. That is God's will. Period. Now let's compare that to how we express our will. The fundamental question to ask yourself is: Do I express and live my will in the pursuit of freedom? Does it emerge from the bliss of unconditionality? When you get an honest answer, don't throw yourself off a cliff. That doesn't solve the anything. Say, "Okay, I get it. I must surrender my willfulness and live in Your will."

We've seen that as soon as individuality takes place, we experience ourselves as not God, but separate. And if we're separate, we inevitably feel we need something to be complete. Remember that we share God's power, but in limited form. So God's desire to express His perfection and joy gets squeezed down into our desire to fulfill some need. We're continually striving to get something, and we always perceive that "something" as existing outside ourselves. Śiva's will is not the desire for anything; it's simply the desire to express His own joy. What a difference in experience!

Śiva's power of knowledge is, "I am all things." Inherent in that Self-awareness is unconditionality, understanding that everything that manifests is being expressed as part of the perfection of the source. Śiva doesn't think, "This is bad, this is good, and that is just mediocre." It's all part of the expression of one state of perfection, without judgment. Śiva simply pulls the trigger and the emission of manifestion bursts forth. Action takes place as the expression of His knowledge that He is all things and all things are Himself. There is no differentiation between Self and non-Self. This is the highest knowledge, born from the capacity of self-reflective awareness.

We are continually trying to control life in order to understand it in the context of our own projections. The mind can never fathom reality, but we're always attempting to fit the infinite into our own level of comprehension. Then we wonder why we don't know the highest truth! Let's work to understand life from Śiva's perspective. We have to go deeper and stop looking where we've been looking because we can never perceive unity from duality.

Looking from a different place means that we stop analyzing everything we think, feel, and do from the level of the mind and emotions. We do not need to micromanage our day, trying to evaluate the meaning or quality of every thought or action. Instead, we become conscious of where they come from. We have been given the power to choose what part of us to engage in and engage from. All thought and action that bind our consciousness to the experience of duality is therefore the willful act of our own ego. We have to raise the level of what we're aware of instead of wondering whether every move we make has any spiritual significance.

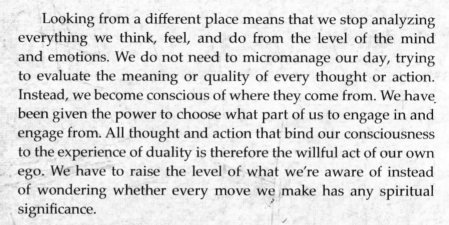

What *does* have significance is being established in an open state. Having our actions arise from openness is a hallmark of doing God's will. Likewise, if we feel contracted, that's a sign that we're only expressing our own will. In many ways, it's that simple—knowing whether we're open or closed. If we focus on opening our hearts instead of letting our awareness become trapped on the surface level of life, we align our consciousness with God's Consciousness, our will with His will. We move past being preoccupied with our own desires, which only surface out of the suffering inherent in our separation from God.

EXERCISING OUR WILL TO BE FREE

Of the veils of duality—I am separate, I am different, I am the doer—it's the first of the three that is most related to our will. We've seen that Siva's will is simply the expression of joy, the act of letting His own effulgence show itself. In us, this infinite power gets condensed down and we end up extending out of ourselves not as an expression of fullness, but in order to fulfill some desire. Then we exercise our individual will to get what we think we need. The reversal of this contraction is the crux of the shift that needs to happen.

The three veils always function together. We've seen that when we feel separate from God we feel incomplete and therefore have the desire for something to fill the void. This translates into willfulness as we plunge ahead into action— usually unconsciously, without regard for the people around us. By perpetual grasping and reaching, we only reinforce the experience of incompleteness.

How many times do we think, "I have to have (fill in the blank) in order to be happy"? When a thought like that comes up, why not let go of it? Instead of feeding that desire, tune back into the unconditional joy that is always available inside. You may have to do that repeatedly, but when you do come in contact with simplicity, joy, and effulgence, there is no reason to reach for anything else. You already have everything.

This is how we align our intention with God's intention, so that we can extend out of ourselves and express our own simple joy. What if every day you sat down and found that simplicity in your heart? What if you then engaged from that fullness as you meet what appears to be the complexity of your life? All the complication, all the troublesome conditions in your life would be infused with simplicity. If we want to find that inner clarity we have to look deeper than our own limitations. We have to ask, "Please free me from my misunderstanding."

The trick is that we have to ask again and again, because just when we think we have the answer, some perfect situation shows up to test if we're *really* free from misunderstanding. So when we encounter a challenge, instead of wishing we could be rid of it or trying to control the outcome, we must learn to trust. We stop ourselves from repeating the mantra of doubt: "God, you are not giving me the life that I believe I deserve." Free from doubt, trusting God, we truly begin to live in the knowledge that if we need something in our life it will be there. This enables us to be fully engaged in enjoying and responding to whatever *is* in our life—and to be grateful, because it's what Śiva gave us. And, guess what? We can be equally grateful for what's not in our life, because if it's not there, we don't need it.

Due to the pressures we face in our complicated world, people often think they have to simplify their lives in order to be quiet and to know themselves. That may be a good place to start, but what we do or how much we do is not the point. Believe it or not, Śiva doesn't care about the specifics of our lives. We get to choose what we do with our will and energies. Being a doctor, lawyer, or Indian chief, or living in a cave doesn't really have any effect on our freedom. We can get lost in the decision to be this or that, or we can be freed in the same decision. In that sense it doesn't make a difference what we do as long as we choose to be open while we're doing it.

free from doubt, trusting god, we truly begin to live in the knowledge that if we need something in our life it will be there

Rudi lived in New York for the explicit purpose of absorbing the intense energy of that city. Perhaps not everyone has Rudi's capacity to devour life, but we shouldn't think that action, per se, is a barrier to experiencing the depth of our consciousness. When we ask, "May I know You as my Self," we're not seeking union with a cute picture of baby Jesus or even with a fierce image of Śiva or Parā. We're saying, "May I know *all of life* as my Self. May I engage in the intercourse of life and not get caught in the duality of it." Rudi, in fact, often said: "If there's a harder way, show it to me. It must be wonderful." How many of us are prepared to repeat that mantra? We're all so busy feeling sorry for ourselves, for how hard life already is, that we're not about to ask for it to be harder. But Rudi's only intention was to dissolve every barrier within himself so that he could grow. To do that, he was willing to engage with anything and everything that required him to consciously break down tension, convert it into energy, and use that power to feed his psychic mechanism.

Whatever dynamics we encounter in our own lives, we must use the power of choice, the power of our will, to penetrate through the experience of living in duality. Parā is the doorway to Śiva. This means that surrendering our will into her will is *our* doorway into God. But letting go of ourselves does not happen by simply writing "I surrender my will" on a chalkboard a thousand times. We have been given the self-reflective capacity to know our own energy and consciousness. When we know what level we function from, we must then choose to transform it. True change requires the deepest surrender because there is enormous

rudi often said: "if there's a harder way, show it to me. it must be wonderful"

effort and struggle involved in transmuting our will from being an instrument of fulfilling some limited desire, to being an expression of a higher will. Without surrender, we are dominated by our egos and change simply doesn't happen.

When we serve Parā and her divine energies, we are choosing to free ourselves by aligning ourselves with Śiva's grace. Not only are we awakening the power of *parā kuṇḍalinī* within us, we're serving that same power as that arousal happens. In other words, it's not *our* power that we're awakening, it's hers, and our own practice is in service to that higher power. Get past the idea that attainment of liberation is a personal acquisition. Ultimately, it's not even our own wish for liberation that guides us. It's Śiva's wish, breathing into us the awareness that we can know Him. This is why it's said that only Śiva frees—and yet we have to respond to grace in order for that to happen. This is why we serve.

sutra ten

the upayas—the means to liberation—are an
ascending capacity to serve the goddess shakti.

Tantric tradition defines the *upāyas* as the means to liberation, but we can also investigate how they outline our expanding capacity to serve. The *upāyas* describe how we focus the energies of our consciousness to serve God, using His own energies, which are the powers of Śakti. We could sum up the progression of the *upāyas* this way: The further we are from God, the more work we have to do, and the closer we are to God, the more work He does.

The four *upāyas* are:

- *Āṇavopāya*—the path of individual effort

- *Śāktopāya* (shaktopaya)—the path of energy

- *Śāmbhavopāya* (shambhavopaya)—the path of awareness

- *Anupāya*—no path, simply living as God

Anupāya is perhaps better described as a state of awareness rather than a means. It is unique in that it does not require meditation or service, because one's individuality is instantly dissolved by divine grace. In one moment of receiving *śaktipāta* directly from God, or with one glance or word from the guru, we recognize our highest Self in a flash. There is no path at all at this point, because we are directly experiencing "I am Śiva." Once that happens, Śiva is the only doer and there is nothing for the *sādhaka* to do. This is the highest of the *upāyas*, but it is only the experience of very few individuals.

For the rest of us, one or more of the *upāyas* may be the predominant strategy we utilize at any given time, but our work is not linear. We don't graduate from *āṇavopāya* and then go on to *śāktopāya*. All of the *upāyas* function together, depending what we are doing and where we are doing it from, but the nature of each *upāya* may shift as as our consciousness changes and we engage them from a higher level. The *upāyas* are like an upward spiral, with the *sādhaka* employing a more refined level of effort, energy, and awareness as he or she progresses.

you can think of the upayas as an upward spiral, with the sadhaka employing a more refined level of effort, energy, and awareness as he or she progresses

ANAVOPAYA: THE PATH OF EFFORT

The reason we start with *āṇavopāya* is that it's the easiest means, even though it looks like the hardest. *Āṇavopāya* is the path of doing, of serving in the world, and it is the path of learning to choose what we really want in life. As we begin our *sādhana*, our experience is one of living in diversity, a long way from God. We feel the effect of living without a connection to God as dissatisfaction or a lack of completeness. So we approach a teacher and begin the spiritual practices given to us, designed to cut through our separation and open us to higher consciousness.

Traditionally, if you went to a guru in India or Tibet and asked to be a student—if you stated, " I want to find God"—the result was that you were handed a pick and asked to dig in the field for twelve years. It was only those individuals who came back again, after all those years of doing manual work, that were accepted to practice with the teacher. This initiation period forced the potential students to ask themselves, "How serious am I?" It instilled self-discipline in each person, as well as the ability to surrender their ideas of what having a teacher and knowing God should be like.

In an ashram setting we learn to serve a community even if we don't get much overt thanks for what we do. We cultivate both our internal and external capacities to serve, and discover that they're never separate. Those who were asked to dig ditches developed not only physical muscle but the muscle of surrender as well. Then, as they began to do the higher practices and the teacher specifically asked them to surrender themselves, they were prepared. By the time we each reach the moment of surrendering our individuality, of completely letting go of all separation from God, if we haven't developed the muscles of surrender, we will hold on to our limited identity.

My son is a world champion martial artist. He spent ten years working intensely to prepare himself to win that title, in a match that consisted of just five three-minute rounds. Those years of practice gave him the capacity to achieve his goal, even though the final bout lasted only a brief amount of time. Make no mistake: those ten years were all devoted to an arduous discipline, consisting of ten hours a day of training. This was the effort needed to develop the capacity to achieve what he wanted.

His success depended on his will and clarity of intention as much as on his technical skill in the ring.

For us, discipline and service have everything to do with knowing what we want in this life and being willing to do whatever we have to do to get it—not what we *want* to do. Focusing on the highest is the primary conscious choice we must make in our *sādhana*. We're always attempting to transform our consciousness, and most of that necessitates letting go of what we think our awareness is. We break through the shell of limitation, of ideas such as, "This is what I understand, and this is what I'm willing to do." We're developing the psychic muscles to direct our awareness through our resistance, our limited understanding, and our self-perpetuating patterns and contractions. *Anavopāya* is the process of creating this inner discipline, which then must be expressed in the world as the willingness to do.

GOD IS THE ONLY DOER

The path of effort centers around the external action of serving the dynamics we're already involved in. We learn to get past our resistance by choosing to do so, by penetrating through whatever misunderstanding exists in us. All of the *upāyas* are our response to grace, to something deeper in us asking to go home. God *is* calling us home, but most people do experience that it takes an enormous amount of effort and focusing of their awareness and energies to simply see beyond the apparent duality of day-to-day life. As we move back into ourselves and begin to have some deeper knowing and a deeper intention for our wish, we're penetrating back through the levels of obscuration and limitation that we normally function under.

We've discussed that Śiva's triadic powers, Parā, Parāparā, and Aparā, are our powers. We can get caught in them, or we can use them to reveal the source of our life. Śiva's powers create all manifestation as well as the force of concealment that seems to shroud our consciousness and prevent us from even having a glimpse of unity. In *āṇavopāya*, we start to take those energies and turn them back inside to discover the truth about ourselves. *Āṇavopāya* is the domain of Aparā, the goddess of action. She's very fierce because she needs to cut through the density of our misunderstanding to reveal a higher awareness.

The act of serving when we don't want to is the training we demand of ourselves to learn how to truly give. That surrender prepares us for the moment when we realize that Śiva is the only doer, and we offer ourselves into His power. Even in *āṇavopāya*, when we perhaps have no awareness of the veil of doership, we're beginning to free ourselves of it. To truly serve, whether digging in the field or working in the bakery, we have to be willing to be put in a situation where we are not doing what we want to do. We only want to sit at the feet of the guru, throw flowers, and do whatever we anticipated would happen when we walked into the presence of a teacher. So we have to take the energy of Aparā, the power of action, and use it to discover the highest in ourselves by serving in whatever way is required.

anavopaya is the domain of apara, the goddess of action. she's fierce because she needs to cut through the density of our misunderstanding to reveal a higher awareness

We have to free our innate deeper consciousness from everything that binds it. If you really serve in the state of *āṇavopāya*—if you really suspend what you think you ought to be doing, and just do for others—it will crunch your bones and grind up every density within you. We're serving God by taking the power of action that He has given to us and reversing its direction back inside so that *it* can return to its source. Not many people can skip over this phase of practice. Those muscles that we build, the strength we forge in the arduousness of just doing whatever is asked of us, is a vital foundation for the other *upāyas*.

Through our efforts, we see past all the difficulty and begin to truly experience gratitude for the possibility of serving and surrendering to God's will. We affirm what is most important to us and what we want to have happen in our life. We understand that if we choose to live in joy and know God, we may have to serve in a capacity that is beyond our conception of what we want to do. The power inherent in that depth of surrender works like a Roto-Rooter, clearing out all impurities, breaking down all resistance within us.

While we serve in the world, we also do whatever meditation practice is given to us by the teacher. This is all part of learning to focus our awareness, bringing it out of its incessant projection and tuning it back inside, beginning to internalize energy. Both inner and outer work penetrate into our psychic body, removing the obscuration and density that doesn't allow our life force to merge back into its source. We feel that blockage as resistance—as our tensions and patterns, as our constant complaining, reaching,

we have to free our innate deeper consciousness from everything that binds it

always have to be careful

and projecting—but we understand that what's happening in our life is a reflection of not living from our highest awareness. So we take the energy we're caught up in and pull it inside, allowing that force to move back up through the *suṣumṇa*, dissolving the impurities lodged in the chakras and in the *granthi*, creating enough space in that central channel so that the full force of *kuṇḍalinī* can rise up. This is how we serve *parā kuṇḍalinī's* desire to merge back into Consciousness, in the heart-space.

Through *āṇavopāya*, we're shifting our awareness of why we're performing action. We take our limited capacity to act, internalize its power, and transform it into the supreme power of action by letting Parā reveal herself in us. And whether that takes twelve years or twelve days, what is transformed is our experience. We change from "I'm doing something" to "I'm allowing this energy to reveal itself." In the process, all our resistance turns into commitment, which turns into more service.

The form or venue that *āṇavopāya* takes place in is not relevant. It may or may not be in the context of a spiritual community under the guidance of a guru. But if you're lucky you will find yourself in a dynamic that requires you to break down your boundaries. No level of work is service if we're doing it and grumbling at the same time. All that action is not achieving its purpose of turning us inside. Having said that, this does not mean that you will not— and that I did not in my own practice—meet extreme resistance to doing. We only complete the work of *āṇavopāya* when we learn to stop complaining. Become grateful for and function from the understanding: This is freeing me from my limitations, from my inability to give and serve. Fundamentally, it's freeing you from your focus on yourself.

SHAKTOPAYA: THE PATH OF ENERGY

Once we can do that inner work with simplicity, grace, and gratitude, we begin to shift into *śāktopāya*. We've made enough contact with the vital force of *kuṇḍalinī* that we can now really focus on uncovering the awareness of life as energy. The genius of Rudi's teaching was his focus on cultivating the experience of flow. In all those years of working in the bakery I was really doing one thing: connecting myself to and establishing myself in that flow, both externally and internally. As I did that, I discovered that the very purpose of my service was to learn to engage every moment of that effort as an energetic flow.

all of life is shakti, and our spiritual practices give us the capacity to be open to it and to be opened by that energy

All of life is *śakti*, and our spiritual practices give us the capacity to be open *to* and opened *by* that energy. We take all the density and resistance that we find as we meet some request to serve, and we breathe it in. We're opening our heart, creating some space inside, and putting the energy of our resistance into the flow. Burning that density and tension allows us to continue to extend and engage life from a different perspective. We begin to see that every dynamic we come across, in ourselves and in the people around us, is simply energy that is either in motion, or dense and not moving.

When we're focused on flow, even a situation that's extremely tense is no longer something we want to run away from. If we open our heart to something and feel its energy, we can engage it and remain open. As soon as we close, we are using that same energy to fight with that dynamic. We have to open deeply as we engage whatever we've been asked to do. Then, the resistance that the mind comes up with—all the complaining, moaning, and focusing on our own needs—becomes energy that we can absorb. As we shovel more fuel into the flow in us, that force starts to dissolve the density of that very dynamic. In *śāktopāya*, serving is about being truly aware that life is energy and that every time we give, the real result is that we're creating a bigger capacity for expanded consciousness in ourselves.

SERVING ENERGY AND KNOWLEDGE

Rudi's own spiritual awakening started when he was a boy, when a cadre of Tibetan lamas would visit him at night, imparting the gift of higher knowledge. These visitations went on for a year, and throughout that time a clear message was conveyed to Rudi: You must serve in order for this gift to flower. Pretty amazing for a young child! Rudi got the message early, but as a young adult, just to be sure, the instruction was sent to him again. While he was meditating Rudi experienced God sitting right in front of him, saying, "You're here to serve—and always remember you're not serving the world, you're here to serve Me." Rudi was being asked to serve the energies and powers of God's own will. The final words from the voice were, "You must teach until the day you die." And that's exactly what he did. He was teaching, up to the moment his plane crashed into the side of a mountain.

In my estimation Rudi was a truly great saint. However, by his own admission, as he was growing he met tremendous internal resistance and, like anyone else, encountered his unwillingness to keep giving after he thought he had given enough. Rudi had a lot to deal with personally. He was born out of hatred and lived through the Depression, but he would not allow anything to lessen his focus on finding freedom and serving others. We each face our own level of density, the different degrees of covering we have to deal with. Perhaps it would be easier for us if God descended and spoke to us directly, but understand: He *is* there at every moment, giving us the feedback we need. We just need to tune past the noise in our heads long enough to hear Him.

Śāktopāya is about serving the energy, and in order to do that we must devour that which consumes energy. Our mind is continually subverting our capacity to open and serve. It is perpetuating the experience of duality, and thought-construct is the binding agent of that experience. The mind is always defining things in terms of separation and difference, and the energy of our own life force is trapped in those thought-constructs. We therefore have to release that energy, pour it into a state of flow, and free it from the veil of illusion. This is how we escape from a limited capacity of perspective and see from a higher place.

Śāktopāya can also be described as the path of knowledge, of serving the goddess Parāparā. We're transforming limited knowledge into the expanded knowledge that life is energy. Our life is not our thoughts, our tensions, or our needs—not anything but different dimensions and currents of energy. In *śāktopāya*,

shaktopaya is about serving the energy, and in order to do that we must devour that which consumes energy we deepen our understanding that the purpose of our actions, the energies we're expressing in life, is to know ourselves. As we engage in the world we're really engaging with a flow of energy, so that we can discover the source of all energy, which is Consciousness. Śakti is the creative power of Śiva, and Her energy leads us back to Him.

When we experience life as energy, we know ourselves to be energy as well. We're more than just our mind, body, or feelings. There is the understanding: I am my *suṣumṇa*, I am this flow of energy. As we experience that vital force in ourselves and extend it into our interaction with life, we begin to experience unity in diversity. We know that everything is simply the energy of God. It may have a varying density, rate of flow, and flavor to it, but it's all one energy, expressed as multiplicity.

The shift from *āṇavopāya* to *śāktopāya* allows us to be engaged in diversity but not be confused by it. We no longer see objects as being like discrete bumper cars, smashing into each other. There is a dynamic and a flow between everything. We stop using energy to try to control life because we have entered into the depth and level of our own practice where we use energy only to dissolve limited knowledge.

SHAMBHAVOPAYA: THE PATH OF AWARENESS

Śāktopāya prepares us for the simple state of Presence of *śāmbhavopāya*, the path of awareness. It's the path of living in God's will, the path of Parā. Because we have surrendered our attempt to use energy in self-service, we have been freed from limited need and will. We have collected all these energies and dynamics of our life and have offered them into the *suṣumṇa*, and back to God. In *śāmbhavopāya*, we acknowledge that our life is Śiva's gift to us, and we're willing to simply ask Him, "What do You want me to do with this life?" Furthermore, we are finally ready to hear God's response: "I want you to enjoy yourself, to experience bliss, and to live in unconditionality. This is My will."

In the state of *śāmbhavopāya* there is no sense of resistance or even separation in offering to do what God wants. We have surrendered into His will to the extent that we only know, "I *am* doing what You want. I am Your instrument for doing." What a subtle, but important difference! We are serving Parā, the one who serves the One. This is an experience of a powerful, palpable energy. Serving God's will is not separate from our own will, but rather the result of the merging of the two. We can do anything, because God's power, flowing through us, is the energy of creation itself.

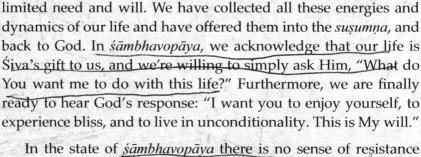

in the state of
shambhavopaya
there is no sense
of resistance or
even separation in
offering to do
what god wants

At this point we understand that none of those energies of action, knowledge, and will are ever separate from the other, even if sometimes one is more in focus. Ascending through the *upāyas* is parallel to ascending back up the *tattvas*. Once we've penetrated the veils of duality the predominant experience is one of pure joy and Presence. We live and experience that Presence as God's Presence, which is not different than our own. Freed from the veil of separation, the mantra *Aham*, "I am," repeats us.

Abhinavagupta wrote a wonderful description of service in *śāmbhavopāya*. He said, "People, occupied as they are with their own affairs, normally do nothing for others. The activity of those in whom every stain of phenomenal existence has been destroyed, and are identical with Bhairava, full of Him, is only benefitting the world."

This tells us unequivocally that there is never a disconnect between our own freedom, the state of living in the simple essence of God's Presence, and our engagement with the world. We are never attempting to reject or run away from anything but only to connect with life from the highest awareness in ourself. This is a central element of the Tantric canon. Any other attitude would be saying that our experience of living in God's Presence is separate from everything else in life. But how could there be any separation, when there is only unity in all of existence? Learning to experience this truth is a powerful, difficult lesson, but it's the key to our liberation. God is manifesting and expanding His freedom through each of us. This is God's purpose; knowing that for ourselves is the purpose of our lives.

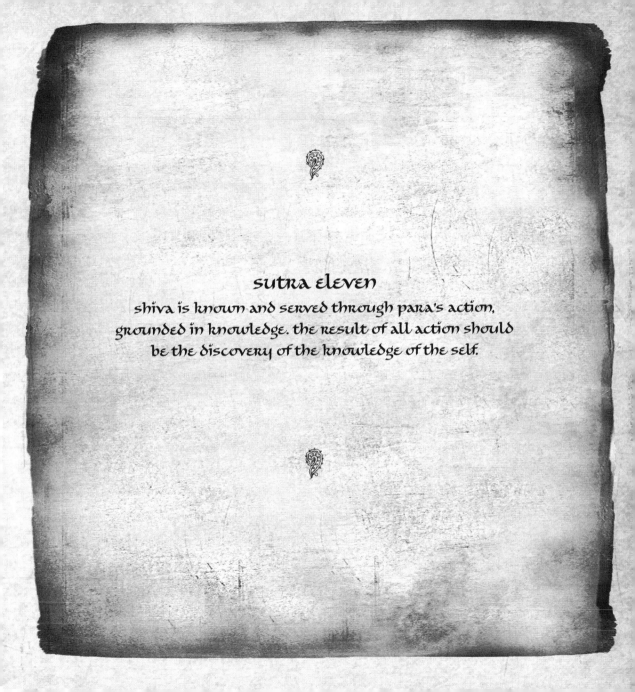

SUTRA ELEVEN

shiva is known and served through para's action,
grounded in knowledge. the result of all action should
be the discovery of the knowledge of the self.

In our *sādhana*, we use various meditation techniques that are fundamental for our growth, and it's of utmost importance that we use them to make contact with a deeper awareness on a daily basis. We meditate in order to penetrate through our internal duality, through the sense of separateness, to find unity. But having this experience during meditation is not enough. Tantric practices enable us to understand the oneness of reality in *every* dimension of our experience—by discovering and establishing ourselves in a new inner resonance and then extending that fullness out into life. As we find the same resonance in what appears to be duality, one infuses the other. This is where our spiritual growth becomes real. It is integrated and even validated in our own experience.

Our action should be for the purpose of reinforcing our knowledge of our highest Self and discovering that Self in all things. Sadāśiva means, "I am all things." That doesn't just mean, "I am all things when I have my eyes closed," but, "I am all things as I engage multiplicity." The very purpose of that engagement is to find that there is no distinction between us and the world, only unity. So instead of performing action in order to get something, we seek to discover that truth.

Of course, there are many levels of truth, and as we attempt to find the highest, part of the grace of *sādhana* is that we uncover the not-so-highest in ourselves. Although it's often a painful revelation, a necessary part of growth is that we discover where our actions are actually coming from. We see that our actions are usually extended and expressed out of our tensions and patterns, and out of our self-serving will. The world is our mirror and when we look at our reflection and see something ugly, it's painful to acknowledge that we haven't been functioning from our highest, and have not been truly serving.

Recognizing the part of us that functions from its own hidden agenda is the first step. Seeing it, we have a choice about how we react. We can get dramatic and feed a sense of guilt or shame with the thought-constructs: I should have, I could have. Or, we can feel gratitude for the possibility of understanding the truth about our nature. Your commitment to service will put up many mirrors, revealing to you what you're really doing, who you're really serving. When you see your limitations, start by joining Kuṇḍalinī Anonymous and admit: "I have an ego." With this knowledge, you have the opportunity to change. That self-reflective capacity of consciousness that we've been given allows each of us to recognize, "All of my actions have been expressed out of my tensions and patterns, and I want to stop that."

Śiva's powers of Consciousness, bliss, will, and knowledge extend into the fifth power, the capacity to act. These powers are the same as the first five *tattvas*, the unmanifest energies contained within Śiva that explode into manifest form. Unfortunately for us, as they express themselves and get further from their source, there is a greater possibility of misunderstanding. That's why so much of our experience of life is that of perceiving only multiplicity and functioning in duality.

We've seen that there is both internal and external duality. When we use our meditation to turn inside we do see our thoughts and we have to work to get past them, but it's easy to understand that all that is part of the one thing called "me." However, when we open our eyes it's harder to escape the perception that there's me, the various dimensions of me, plus "them" and all the dimensions of them. Our confusion just multiplies!

Nityananda said, "Look for the One in the many." That means in our engagement with the world, we have to penetrate through multiplicity to find unity. Freedom is exactly that: seeing the One in the many. What more powerful way of realizing this than to consciously use our action, our engagement in this world, for that discovery? And as we come to experience that all of life is one thing—that all these people are really *me*, really God—then what choice do we have but to serve them? Now flip that question: What does it feel like when we don't do that? If we recognize others as God, and instead of giving, loving, and serving them we choose to be focused on ourself, what are we saying?

nityananda said, "look for the one in the many"

DESIRE CREATES KARMA

Due to our misunderstanding, Śiva's universal free will, intended only to express and share the joy of His existence, contracts into desire. Our individual experience of divine action becomes very narrow in focus and most of our actions are only for the purpose of getting a result or having something. Due to this, desire turns into action that produces karma, reinforcing our patterns of need. That desire for something, and the grasping that results from it, perpetuates our experience of being incomplete. It's an endless hunger that is continually expressed in all of our actions. This is how the divine will inherent within us shrinks into personal, self-serving will.

Karma is the end result of acting from limited knowledge. It's impossible to say, "I'm going to stop creating karma," but we *can* say, "I'm going to stop performing the actions that create karma." It's a matter of penetrating back through our actions to understand where the karma comes from—namely, desire. And desire arises when we function from a place that feels separation and doesn't know how to do anything else except keep reaching for something to fill the empty space. That's why we talk about knowledge: we're looking at the source to understand why we act in a limited way. Then, because we see *why* we act out of desire, we can change. As difficult and painful as it is to stop reaching and grasping, that is exactly what we must do.

karma is the end result of acting from limited knowledge

By serving, and by changing our awareness, we ask to break our patterns. We affirm our intention to not let that same level of misunderstanding be the source from which our actions are expressed. We engage in action to discover that we no longer need to get anything out of it. One of the main themes of the Bhagavad Gītā is surrendering "the fruit of all action." That's really another way of saying, "Thy will be done. May I do what is wanted and needed by God, not by me." So sit down and ask God, "Show me how to serve You." And when you open your eyes and encounter all the people in your life, don't say, "Sorry, God, that's not what I meant. Can You show me an easier way to serve?"

SEVA IS KARMA-FREE ACTION

People get very confused about service. Questions come up that reflect self-doubt or lack of clarity about how, when, and why to give. So let's be practical: Just serve. Give what's needed. Let go of the incessant focus on yourself and start doing. If, as you engage in the world, an uncomfortable truth about yourself arises—namely that you haven't been acting from the highest level—don't run away to a cave. That would be like saying, "I've seen the light and I don't really like it. I don't want to look in the mirror anymore."

Through our capacity to see our own state, we understand that our service is conditional and that it's reinforcing our own internal duality. Perhaps we have been doing something out of fear, or only to please the teacher or someone important in our life. If we *can* keep looking in the mirror long enough, if we're willing to recognize the limited experience that we're creating for ourself, then we have the possibility of penetrating through our self-absorption. This includes asking to find situations in which we have to serve without condition. Then we're in the process of doing exactly what we say we want—discovering the truth of our own Self, and the knowledge that we can give and serve without thought of price.

We may still have questions such as: Am I functioning from my ego, or offering true service? My position is that it's better to serve even if it's from ego than not serve and be constantly grabbing. At least we're training our muscles to do something different. We're learning to tune our awareness away from selfishness and willfulness, and even if our motivation isn't the purest, at least it's been filtered a little bit. Changing how and why we act doesn't mean we become inactive, so one could argue that every time we act there's *something* that's produced as a result. Why would we act if we don't want something to take place? So serving unconditionally and without attachment is really a matter of where that action arises from.

If we're honest with ourselves, we see that when we do things, especially when we start to reach for something, it's usually an unconscious act. We have an idea, we don't exactly know where it comes from, and we just go do it. And unfortunately, we often find ourselves somewhere over the edge of a cliff as a result. It's not until we're in freefall that we think, "Maybe this wasn't such a good idea." Like Wiley Coyote in the cartoons, perpetually trying to catch the Roadrunner, we reach for something, and just as we're about to grab it, we're six feet out into space. Wiley doesn't seem to learn from his experience, and mostly, neither do we.

Unconscious action does not refer to walking from one room to the next or driving to the store. These actions are not binding.

We're talking about the actions that come from our suffering, from our misunderstanding that we need something outside of ourself in order to be happy. We each have a God, whether it's money, sex, power, or whatever else we fixate on. It's not getting or having those things that's the problem; it's only our attachment to needing them that binds us. When action radiates out from that state of bondage, we're perpetually looking outside to become full, reinforcing the very experience that the binding created in the first place.

When we get attached to chasing after needs, we're really just numbing ourselves to our own fundamental pain, caused by our separation from God. That's what most people do, even though they're not aware of it. We regularly read stories about some extremely wealthy person, with everything in their life, who is still deeply unhappy. Yet some part of us believes: When *I* have all that, I won't feel this pain. For some period of time, that may even be true. And that's okay . . . but what are we after? Temporary happiness, or freeing ourselves from the pangs of separation?

liberation from the misunderstanding of separation is imperative

The fact that we *do* experience the pain of separation is a gift from God. Otherwise we might be like zombies walking around on the earth, bumping into walls, doing every crazy thing known to man. But grace enables us to experience our own state, and that's why Rudi always said, "Pain is God loving you." We have that feedback to tell us that something is wrong. The challenge for us as *sādhakas* is to penetrate through "another boyfriend just broke up with me," to the real source of that experience. We're focusing our awareness, choosing to look beyond the bumps and scratches of everyday life and find the part of us that is free from pain and doesn't need healing.

Liberation from the primary misunderstanding of separation is imperative. It's so important to understand that whatever we're doing, our action should be focused on *that*. We're trying to move from action back into the knowledge of "I am all things. I am complete." And once we have that, we just extend back out— and now it doesn't matter what we have or don't have because we're free of our attachment and our need for anything. Another wonderful quote from the Bhagavad Gītā describes this state: "He whose mind is not agitated in the midst of sorrow, who although surrounded by pleasure is free from longing, from whom passion, fear, and anger has disappeared—he is said to be a sage." This is the knowledge of the Self.

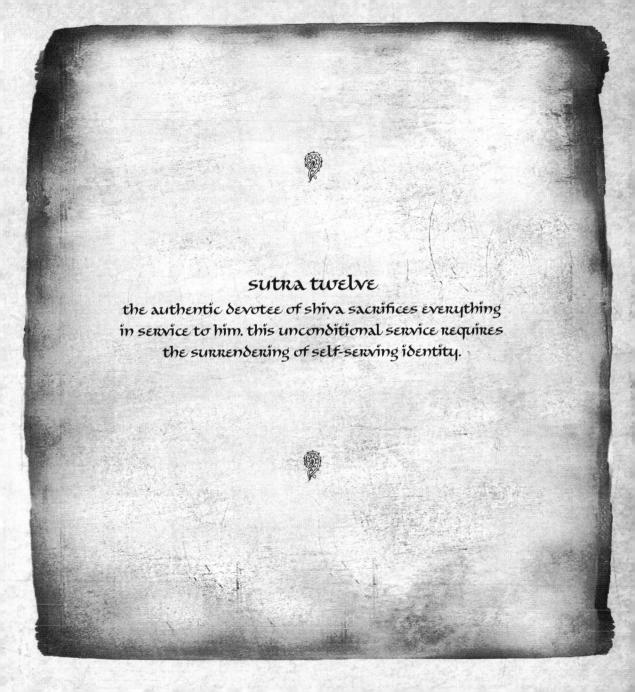

sutra twelve

the authentic devotee of shiva sacrifices everything
in service to him. this unconditional service requires
the surrendering of self-serving identity.

When you enter into a lawsuit, there's a phase called "discovery," which is the collection of proof to defend your position. I find it so interesting that every discussion about service seems to center around what service is *not*. We seek to prove to ourselves that we can remain as we are, not needing to stretch beyond our limitations. We ask: How can I not have to serve? If I'm doing this and this, isn't that good enough? And please don't use that word "surrender," so I'm not reminded that I have to offer myself unconditionally—because only then can I feel comfortable.

The discussion of identity is the same. There's the perpetual defense of, "This is my identity, this is not my identity. If this is God's identity, how can it be my identity?" It's a mental Ping-Pong match that demonstrates that understanding life as an individual is the source of bondage. Because our perception is based in duality, we can only have a dualistic experience, and so much of the time our perception and projections are our way of proving our own truth. We are continually reaching to fill an internal void, holding on to what we know, and trying to fit all the context of life into that small container.

Even though we theoretically understand that living as God is the source of freedom, there's such intense fear involved in letting go of our own identity. We're not necessarily thinking, "I'm fearful of surrendering myself"—we're just not doing it. We perpetually project our experience of life from our perception of separateness. There's a background conversation in our minds that sounds like: "I'm John and I'm doing this, I'm John and this happened to me, I'm John and I'm doing this with/to these people." All our inputs and outputs are filtered through this viewpoint.

SURRENDERING INTO GOD'S PERSPECTIVE

It's really the sacrificing of this mind-set that is at the heart of our conscious choice to let go. We have to transcend our self-centered thinking and stop trying to understand life from that perspective. Instead, we ask, "May I understand from God's perspective." But so often, when we even start to consider surrendering our identity, a little contraction creeps in. That's the resonance of fearing the loss of identity, and we feel it viscerally. Personal identity is very entrenched in us.

Our interaction with life tends to be focused on perpetuating and defining our limited identity, which is one of being in relation *to* something else. In other words, the world is not only the object of our own experience but every experience we have is in relation to it. We're constantly concerned with how everything affects or doesn't affect us. We even think we're separate from our own life, and we're always trying to change it—insisting that if "that life out there" was different, *we* would be different.

Perhaps the greatest thing that could happen to us would be that our life never changed. What a drag that would be! That would require a lot of surrender! It would require that we shift our experience so that it isn't in relation to anything, but from within us, encompassing what we engage. Then, there would be no separation, no longer an object of our awareness to blame for our unhappiness. We'd see that everything arises from inside us and that nothing needs to change except our consciousness. Letting go of defining ourselves in relationship *to* anything, our true identity is revealed. We are simply a servant of God.

If we're honest with ourselves, we notice when we're not functioning from that highest consciousness. We recognize that feeling separate from God, from our life, and from other people only reinforces the notion that there's something "other" that will change our experience. So we choose to sacrifice the ego by not feeding its energy and not engaging from it. We simply tune our awareness out of dualistic thinking, thereby surrendering all limited personal perspective into God's perspective. This is how *we* change, without requiring that our life change.

perhaps the greatest thing that could happen to us would be that our life never changed

DEPTH OVER TIME

Rarely does the atom bomb explode in spiritual life. It's not like we're instantly free, duality is obliterated, and the ego no longer has any grip on us. Most change happens day by day, as we create a little more openness, allowing a little more light to show through. This is why Rudi discribed spiritual work as "depth

over time." Those little moments add up to a bigger openness. That's the point of sacrificing our incessant demand that life reinforce our limited perspective. We recognize how our egoic identity has been dominating our awareness and we choose to change. We don't necessarily know what it means to *not* function from ego, but we start to look for the place that does know so that we can act from there. If we let go of "I know it, I got it, I'm gonna do it" long enough to allow another resonance to shine in us, it illuminates a higher awareness. This is a real sacrifice, because we must consciously say "no" to our usual impulse to plunge headlong into actions that are the expressions of ego.

We say we want to surrender the ego, but why do we expect to suddenly be free from it without doing our inner work? We want angels to sprinkle fairy dust on us or a trumpet fanfare to announce the big bang. You will have those internal explosions, but only because you've set off enough little firecrackers in yourself to create an opening. Growth is exponential. It starts small, opens more, and then it keeps expanding. The guided meditations accompanying this book are designed to bring you to the space of *dvādaśānta*, the abode of Parā, God's will. You may not feel it at all at first, but your awareness is reaching for it, allowing you to find it in time. If we don't reach for a different perspective, we're always going to be limited.

In our meditation, we keep feeling and letting go, seeking that deeper awareness. When we can immerse ourselves in that state our heart is open and everything is so simple and joyful. We don't want to stop, because we think that when we open our eyes the experience will fade. That doesn't need to happen, but it tends to do so as long as we function from a perspective of inner and outer, subjectivity and objectivity, me and it. Fortunately, openness is more than a nice feeling we have in meditation; it's a palpable consciousness we can live in. When we consistently engage life from that state, we break the illusion of a boundary between inner and outer. We stop relating to anything as a separate object because we recognize that our own consciousness creates all the people, our job, and every pressure we face in life. We can experience the unity in all that diversity, knowing that nothing is outside of us.

Śiva's experience is that all manifest life extends from His infinite Consciousness, but it is never separate from Him and is always the perfect expression of joy and freedom. Through our *sādhana* we discover that Śiva dwells within us as our Self, and His perspective becomes ours as well. We find that our life is never separate from us because it emerges from *our* consciousness, and we experience that it is perfect. Even life's challenges are created from within us so that we might come to know a higher truth— that we can never ever be the victim of our own life. Any lesser perspective is something we willingly sacrifice.

We've seen that we can never find freedom outside ourselves, in the acquisition of a thing or in some new experience. When we identify with our body, separation between "inside" and "outside" makes sense. Even in the *dvādaśānta* meditation, we might at first feel that space as being outside our body, but it's not outside our consciousness. It's only our bodily perspective that says, "I end here." Energy and awareness are not tied to having a physical body, but that's another limitation we accept as our identity. As we open our heart, it expands past any previously known boundary, opening to an awareness that is not restricted to a physical location. We're opening beyond any limited ability to perceive identity and expanding into God's identity, which already exists, as a reality always known to itself.

The specifics of our life don't necessarily change, but the need for life to change is eliminated. That's why it doesn't much matter what your name is, what your career is, or what exactly you do. It's all about where we do it from, what level of consciousness we are acting in. Established in openness, we don't have to analyze if some activity is our will or God's will. We have repeated the mantra "May my will be Your will," and because we have the capacity to be aware of our state, we can immediately see when we start expressing willfulness.

LETTING GO OF WHAT BINDS US

One common way we exert our will is by trying to change other people. Even an intellectual debate is usually us saying, "This is how *you* should understand things." That may not always be the case, but if we're quiet and watch, we notice that we're generally trying to change people by telling them how things should be. It's a display of arrogance. This doesn't mean we should never have a discussion, but as we grow spiritually we find less need for that kind of talk. Let's be busy truly trying to understand life rather than telling others what their life should be. Within the field of freedom, everything is possible—but what is that energy creating? Is it creating freedom or bondage?

Day by day, we play out that question in mundane but powerful ways that affect people's lives. So much of what we do is battling in the realm of the ego, and it's like trying to rearrange the furniture on the *Titanic*. We fight to change this or that, but guess what? The ship is going down. Authentic *sādhana* requires penetrating through the grip of the ego and being willing to change our experience on the *deepest* level. This focus immediately eliminates so much of the fight of life, the struggle of changing this and that. We're just not focused on any specific conditions of life because we understand that's not what we need to change. And then whether anything changes or not isn't relevant.

Our feeling that we are giving up something when we throw our tensions, needs, and misunderstandings into the fire only demonstrates our incredible attachment to our identity. We define ourselves in terms of how we suffer: I don't deserve, people are always doing things to me, I need this, I don't want that, nobody loves me. That list goes on and on. That's why we must let go of everything that binds us. Self-rejection and self-hatred are particularly deep patterns of binding that are created from within the experience of the ego. While it might be helpful to recognize these patterns and breathe some light and openness into them, we usually fight with our contractions and feed their energy. Then, self-rejection becomes the glue we use to put our identity together. We see people who function from very self-destructive

authentic sadhana requires penetrating through the grip of the ego and being willing to change our experience on the deepest level

places. As they ruin their lives again and again, they reinforce and prove to themselves and to others, "I am not worthy."

Rudi told us so clearly: "You can't hate yourself and love God." You can't engage in a constant struggle with self-rejection, and the self-destructive patterns that come out of that, and expect to change. We have to go inside and find an awareness that doesn't function from that perspective. It may be buried very deeply, which only tells us that we have to dig beneath our self-rejection. From the perspective of the ego, surrender is not possible. The ego only reinforces itself because that's all it knows.

rudi told us so clearly: "you can't hate yourself and love god"

RISING ABOVE THE LEVEL OF EGO

The ego cannot experience unity because it *is* that sense of separate, personal identity. That's why liberation is not a personal acquisition but freedom *from* that limited perspective. As we ask to be freed, we must also respond to the gift of freedom that we've been given. During the guided meditations, we may feel some resistance to surrendering our identity. When we try to offer ourselves into a higher will, we reach the boundary of the part of us that doesn't want to be dissolved. The ego says, "No!" We have to repeat mantras and make commitments to break down this resistance within us, to hold on to what we say we want. This is how we respond to grace.

If we look at the *tattvas, buddhi* is the level of consciousness that has the power to discriminate and to perceive the truth. It's above the limited constraint of mind and ego, which don't have even a crack in them through which to see the light. So we have to penetrate deeper than that, into *buddhi*, an awareness that starts to illuminate what we experience. Think about going into a pitch dark cave. After you've bonked your head on the wall a few times and tripped and broken your leg, you remember to light a candle. Immediately you can see where you want to go. You may not see far enough, so you light more candles until you are no longer stumbling around in the dark.

Meditation is seeing beyond the limited identity we thought of as ourself and finding the place in us that sees itself. Not, "I am this thing here and God is over there," but truly finding God and knowing we are That. Someone once asked Rudi, "Have you seen God?" and he just smiled and said, "Well, I've gotten up to His knees." Part of the grace of God is that if we suddenly saw all of Him it would be overwhelming. The ego can't take that luminous explosion; it contracts too fast in reaction. That's why opening and freeing ourselves from that bondage is a day-by-day experience. But do make sure that's what's happening in your day.

the ego cannot experience unity because it is that sense of separate, personal identity. that's why liberation is not a personal acquisition but freedom from that limited perspective

We want to find enough clarity in the luminosity of choice that describes *buddhi*, and, from there, offer ourselves in service. This is how our intention gets directed at something bigger than ourselves. Your ego will never offer itself in service. We have to sacrifice our ego, but it will kick and scream when we make that offering. Every struggle we encounter—all our grumbling and fighting, all thoughts of "I shouldn't have to do this"—is just the resistance of the ego.

SERVING GOD BY GROWING

Seva may appear to be self-serving in the sense that we consciously use it to find our own higher identity. But there's never a conflict between our growth and serving God. In fact, what higher service to God would there be than to grow bigger than the smallness that is the limitation of God's will? Our growth is the expansion of the freedom within us, so there can never be a conflict. However, real growth is not just found sitting in meditation but in being able to open our eyes and extend ourselves into the life we live. We're serving God's will to expand freedom in ourselves, and positively affecting others at the same time.

There is tremendous power in our commitment to serve. It focuses our awareness and our will on the choice to bring out the highest within us—but we can't repeat the mantras of will and service with sincerity and not have that shake things up. They require that we become very cognizant of what we're doing every day. We can't offer ourselves one day and then say, "never mind" as soon as it's inconvenient. Yet we still choose to serve, knowing our resistance will arise and that we will sometimes find it difficult to live up to our commitments.

Remember, there is also tremendous power in the ego. It's the black hole of consciousness. Consciousness moves beyond time and space, but our ego has the capacity to consume the light of consciousness back into itself. That's why the ego is often called the abode of darkness, and it's why "guru" means "dispeller of darkness," not "bringer of light." The light is already there, but the ego has as much power to obscure reality as consciousness has to reveal it.

The light of Consciousness is always within us. We are that light. It's what we look for when we close our eyes, and what we look for when we open them. We choose our experience in this life. Do not let the ego make that choice for you. It will only create a limited experience instead of one focused on liberation. Sutra One said, "The teachings are meant for those who wish to awaken." When we really see the cost of *not* awakening, then we shudder. Then, we're willing to do whatever it takes to wake up, because the pain of remaining asleep is far greater than the pain of freeing ourselves. So it costs a little. So what? We have to be willing to surrender our identity. Spiritual growth is always dangerous to the ego. Our own consciousness becomes the fire that consumes every personal limitation.

But here's the secret: Our sacrifice can only be made from joy, from our love for God. It can only be made from the deepest part of us that really wants to be free. If we consciously offer ourselves in devotion, then sacrifice is not difficult at all. The gratitude, openness, and joy in that offering are themselves the reward, and that is what encourages us to keep surrendering everything that gets in the way of knowing God. You have to love your life. Any rejection of any part of life is us *not* loving it. And those parts that we don't really love, that won't go away, are there for a purpose—to help us understand something. Seek to understand. Sacrifice the misunderstanding. The discovery period is over, we have our proof, and we realize we're going to lose the case.

the ego has as much power to obscure reality as consciousness has to reveal it

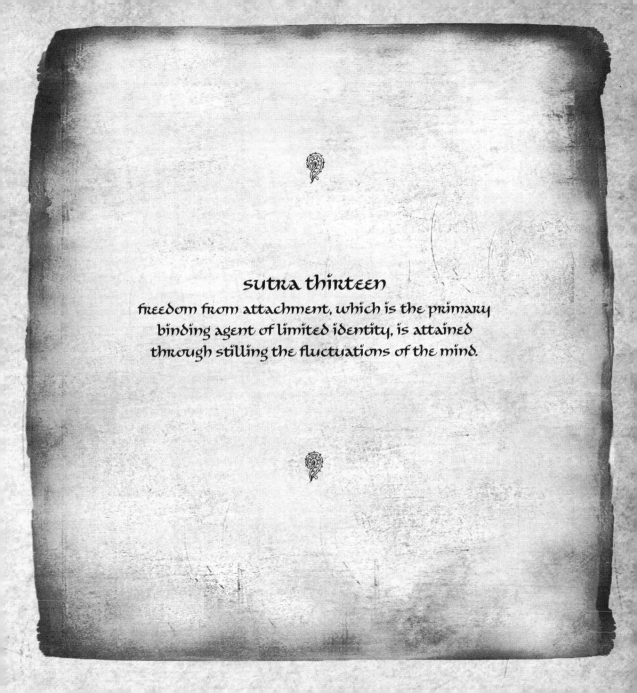

sutra thirteen

freedom from attachment, which is the primary
binding agent of limited identity, is attained
through stilling the fluctuations of the mind.

In real life we don't walk around thinking, "Today, I need to free myself from the veils of duality." We just don't think in those terms. But we do get bogged down in our pain, which gets translated into thoughts, emotions, and needs. We're really struggling with the effects of those veils, and don't realize that the lack of simplicity, stillness, and clarity in our awareness is due to one primary cause: separation.

With self-awareness, we see how separation from God, from our own source, creates the effects we live in and experience from. As we penetrate through the surface reality, the first step is to free ourselves from the grip of that effect. We've discussed how separation ripples out into a feeling of incompleteness, and from that lack, a desire arises to fill the void within us. We start to reach for something, attempting to control life. Because we are experiencing from the perspective of duality, we think the pain we're feeling is due to the engagement we have with our life, and we seek to solve our problems on that level.

This is how our *desire* to be filled becomes the *need* to be filled. Since we act from the perspective of our previous experiences, we keep reinforcing the idea that the incompleteness is going to be satisfied by some object, something outside of ourselves.

Even wanting to be loved by another person is usually a search for wholeness. Personal love is a wonderful and natural thing, but a subtle hunger can creep in, causing misunderstanding. We believe that when we're loved by someone it's going to complete us and put an end to our problems. In this way, we try to escape from the inner knowledge that our pain is caused by something beyond the fact that a particular person doesn't love us.

DESIRE AND DESIRELESSNESS

There's nothing wrong with desire. Śiva's will, the power of Parā, is *His* desire. The fundamental difference is that Śiva's will is the desire to express the freedom and simplicity of His own state. Everything that is imagined and manifested is, from Śiva's perspective, the expansion of completeness. This is very different from the reaching and grasping we do as the expression of some emptiness. Desire binds us because it becomes a need that determines our experience. Desire is responsible for the destruction of the experience of the highest bliss—which is self-sufficient and needs nothing for it to exist.

You can want everything in life. It's fine to want the love of others, financial security, or a beautiful place to live. But if you get confused and allow your experience to be determined by the *need* for that, then you have automatically reinforced the dualistic perspective that, "I am separate, I am not whole, and so I need x, y, or z." The need for something outside of ourself comes from a very deep part of us, and it's always the problem.

Wanting to love God is not the wish for external fulfillment. It's only the discovery of that which already exists within us. This longing we feel is grace. But the sense of wanting to experience unity with God can get altered and misunderstood if we're not looking for God within. When we project this longing, it then gets expressed as the need for something outside of us, and we attach our need to some object. Attachment is the driving force of our experience of need. Like a horse with blinders on, we only have a single focus, and our life is motivated by the urgency to acquire that thing. Then, when we have it, we're afraid to lose it! That's equally as binding as not having it. Instead of the joy of having and sharing, what's functioning is a fear of loss.

The Sufis have a beautiful saying, "Hold on to your life, with an open hand." This is opposed to gripping so hard that we squeeze the juice out of life. The Sufis are describing nonattachment, what Nityananda called desirelessness. Living without attachment or desire is important, but it does not mean moving to the outer reaches of Tibet, living in a cave, and avoiding all the objects that keep us confused. As Tāntrikas, we do not reject life. We consciously engage with the world, precisely to learn when we're *not* engaging from the highest perspective. That self-knowledge is the platform from which we begin to act from a higher place—one that is seeking to discover the unity and fullness of life instead of reinforcing the incompleteness of it.

We're looking for a categorically different experience, including a new ability to choose how we engage life. When a sense of lack motivates how we function, that's the resonance

wanting to love god is not the wish for external fulfillment. it's only the discovery of that which already exists within us

we're going to reinforce. But paradoxically, the resonance also creates the dynamics that give us the opportunity to work through our sense of incompleteness. Then, we have a choice to unconsciously perpetuate that resonance or stop repeating the patterns that reinforce it.

What if we consciously infused our life with simplicity and joy? What if we no longer tried to extract fulfillment from life but, instead, recognized the already-existing fullness of it? Note that "it" means the life that's projected out of our own heart. The problem is that we always seem to want the life that's projected out of somebody else's heart. We think *that* life would be perfect, and we get jealous, pissed off, or blame God for not giving us what we think we need. But here's the thing: You will only find the fullness of life in your own life. You will never find it if you're focused on the lack you perceive. That's looking for the wrong thing, from the wrong place.

THE MIND ALWAYS GETS IT WRONG

Abhinavagupta has emphatically stated, "Thoughts are the source of all bondage." The mind is always trying to define life, and it will always get it wrong. That's why we have to stop trying to understand life from our mind. When we look at the *tattvas* we see that mind (*manas*) arises after one becomes an individual. *Manas* cannot see above its own level, and it's constantly trying to define its experience from within its own boundaries. We literally can't think outside that box!

Our thoughts are continually attached to objects, especially the "objects" in our mind. This is the essential source of our misunderstanding. We've discussed the two dynamics of duality: that we perceive both external and internal separation. External duality—seeing the distinction between things—is fine as long as we use our senses in a strictly observational manner. "Here is a house. That is a person." This is not binding, unless we start attaching or projecting our perception of the house or person, or if we judge them. Then we are defining something instead of perceiving its truth. We think, "Why don't I have the money to buy this house? Am I not good enough? This person is attractive, the other not." We define those objects with our thoughts and they become something we've limited and misinterpreted. In reality, all objects are energy, manifest as form.

As long as we perceive any form to be outside ourselves, external duality leads to problems. But our external duality is really an after-effect of internal duality—our misperception that "I am separate from God." There are "two" in that statement: God and me. This split is the fundamental source of our suffering because it leads us to project *from* duality, through our thoughts, out into all aspects of life. As we've seen, our separation leads us to believe we need something "out there" to complete us, so the never-ending patterns of need and desire dominate our awareness.

in reality, all objects are energy, manifest as form

If your heart is truly open you will have no thoughts and you will live in a desireless state, in the experience of resting in fullness. You must use your awareness to demand to live in a

different place within yourself. Do not accept anything less than opening your heart and letting your mind fall into it. Until you do that, you will suffer from a confusion that is both internal and external in nature. Only the heart can open big enough to experience the simplicity of our divinity. We can't understand higher awareness from a mundane level—but if we understand mundane experience from a higher level then everything is clear. The problem is that we don't believe it's that simple, so we keep pounding on life, constantly manipulating and demanding, and doing everything except truly opening our hearts.

THOUGHTS CREATE BONDAGE

Our thoughts are powerful energies that reinforce our feelings of incompleteness. When Abhinavagupta said that thoughts are the source of all bondage, he did not mean, "Thoughts are bad," since in their own dimension they serve a purpose. If we think, "I have a meeting with my boss today," it's not binding. It's only when we get to the meeting and find that the boss thinks we're not doing a good job that we get into trouble. We fall into a mental tirade of anger or self-rejection and binding takes place.

That's why we attempt to get quieter in our heart, in that dimension of consciousness that isn't projecting and creating objects and then attaching itself to those objects. We want to experience life from God's perspective without the binding thoughts that separate us, the subject, from the objects in our life. Śiva created all objectivity without ever losing the experience that everything is happening within Him. In truth, the same principle applies to us: All of the objects we relate to arise within the field of our own onsciousness. We just think objects are separate. From limited awareness, even other people are seen as "objects" in the sense that we think they're outside of us. But how could something be an object in the field of our consciousness, if we weren't aware of it? It appears to be an object, but we start to understand it's simply an object *within* our consciousness.

Thinking in terms of objects is inherent in the experience of duality, but moving toward unity is never a rejection of life. Although there is no need to deny anything in ourselves, we *can* be aware of how our interaction with objects affects our consciousness. If we find ourselves in the grip of thought-constructs and the arising emotions that accompany them—whether about sex, money, power, or food—we toss them into the fire. We choose what and from where we want to engage.

all of the objects we relate to arise within the field of our own consciousness. we're just not aware of that and think objects are separate

Thoughts are the source of bondage because they create projection and attachment. Let's say we adopted the attitude, "My life is perfect as it is." A sense of stillness and fullness arises, so there is no binding and we don't need to reach or change anything. All other thoughts just stop. But as soon as a new idea pops up, like, "I really need a different job," we immediately shift our focus to that instead of resting in perfection. And then that one thought multiplies into: I need to make these plans, six phone calls, and I need the job to look like this, to do that for me. We now have a multiplicity of thoughts that create a pathway for our energy, and we get lost.

As soon as one thought arises that creates the resonance of "not fullness," we begin to reach. It was just a *thought* of non-fullness, but immediately an energy of need is generated and we start chasing some form that we ourselves create. That form is perceived to be outside of ourselves, and it reinforces the feeling, "I gotta have *that*, in here." It's already *in here*—it came from within us! But that need has arisen, as well as the thought that it's not part of us, and that's what's binding.

It is in our mind that we experience, project, and sustain our sense of lack. The limiting thoughts and emotions that arise out of desire and attachment can easily become dominant in our lives. Anger is one of those powerful emotions and it encases our awareness in limitation, preventing access to higher knowledge. It appears in the senses when we "see something" created in the organs of perception. Anger then enters the mind in the form of our desire to do something, emerging as reaction or projection. Anger is the enemy of freedom in the form of ignorance. A single thought is binding because it builds itself into a range of projections and emotions. It leads to the matrix of thought-construct and becomes fear, anger, self-rejection, and this, and that . . . endlessly. We're just following a trail, getting further and further outside ourselves, and can't find our way back home.

This is why the teachings of the Spandakārikās are so useful. They advise us to center ourselves and tune in to the pulsation of the heart, the pulsation of Consciousness. From there, we allow thought to arise and subside inside the heart, without giving it the energy to extend into form. In this way, we avoid becoming attached to any energy coming from our thoughts. Through this Spandakārikā practice we come to recognize that thoughts arise from a place of separation. We can depersonalize the thought in the sense that we realize there's a deeper source, and this bigger perspective helps us let go of it. We begin to see how the veils of duality ripple out through the *vāsanās*, the latent impressions in us, and cause thoughts to arise. If we allow our thoughts to emerge and subside without acting on them, the energy of thought does not create an outward effect.

When we see that it's only our own thought, perception, and projection that are perpetually insisting that life isn't perfect and something is needed to fill the void, we can flip our understanding. We can avoid getting caught in the attachments we create out of our thought-constructs. This means we have to let go of the sense of need in order to experience fulfillment. That's why *sādhana* requires sacrifice and surrender, and we can find that capacity through our conscious intention to serve. This is what really pulls our awareness out of the fight and struggle of our own need and focuses it on something higher, something bigger than ourselves.

a single thought is binding because it builds itself into a range of projections and emotions

INTERNALIZING OUR ENERGY

This new awareness is like a tether we shoot into our heart—one we can use to pull ourselves back there, even when there's some turbulence that distracts us. We have anchored ourselves in the psychic body. And in the center of the *suṣumṇa* is the internal breath—the divine thread we follow back to its source. As we internalize our energy, our awareness, and our wish, we are pulling back into ourselves all that external focus, even while our eyes are wide open. It's this external gaze and internal focus that dissolves the distinction between "in" and "out."

We must continually focus inside, directing our consciousness toward our heart, the place in us that functions without thoughts. In terms of the *tattvas*, it is in *buddhi* that we can recognize a thought as a limiting construct, and that subtle discerning capacity is expanded to the point that we can perceive from Consciousness itself. As the veils of duality get thinner, we find our heart in *puruṣa*, the individuated expression of Consciousness. It's only awareness itself, unencumbered by thought, that is able to reach past the veils, and that's why we must repeatedly surrender whatever binds us.

our sadhana should be a celebration of life, and even if we have to sacrifice something, it should be a joyous offering

Our *sādhana* should be a celebration of life, and even if we have to sacrifice something, it should be a joyous offering. So while we have to recognize that our thought-constructs are binding, we don't need to pick up a sledgehammer and start whacking on them. We simply let go. We don't follow thoughts to their fruition, to the point where they take the energy of our life force and create form that we become attached to. Form exists; it is the condensation of Consciousness and energy. We didn't create all this form—but we choose how we engage the specificity of form in our life. That relationship is either from a place of thought that's trying to define it, or a place of openness and simplicity that recognizes it as the expression of God's own effulgence.

Thought-constructs are the weave we use to create and perpetuate dualistic perception. In the experience of unity we still perceive diversity, but it is consumed within the awareness that "I am all things." Once we experience oneness inside us, where could that end? Diversity no longer consists of objects outside of ourself, limited by our definition and projection. *Nirvikalpa samādhi* means a thought-free state. In the state of liberation we simply experience Consciousness expressing itself. Nothing is binding on our awareness or diminishing our experience of oneness by dividing it into separate categories.

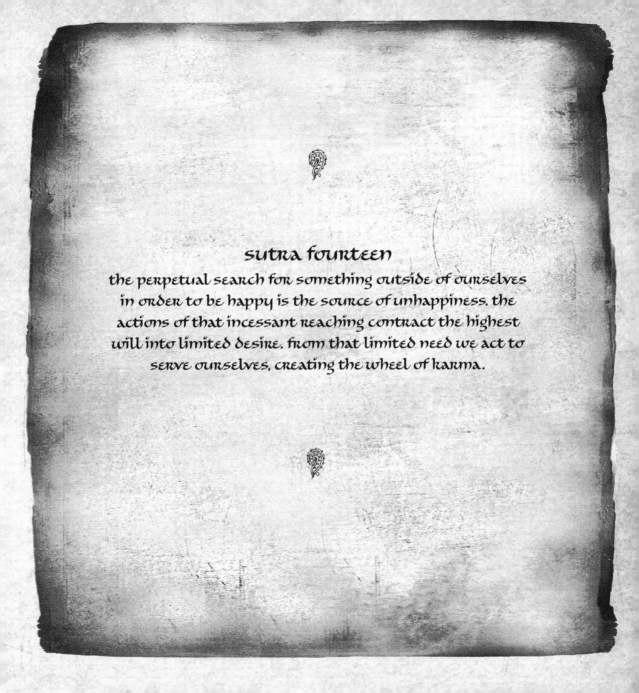

sutra fourteen

the perpetual search for something outside of ourselves
in order to be happy is the source of unhappiness. the
actions of that incessant reaching contract the highest
will into limited desire. from that limited need we act to
serve ourselves, creating the wheel of karma.

Aparā is the goddess of action, the vibrating potency of Śiva. This is the power that creates all of life out of Śiva's Consciousness. From within the bliss of His own perfection, the will to create, and the knowledge of how to express it, comes the explosion into being of the very power we also function from. When we tune in to that during our meditation we merge with Aparā's supreme power of action and begin to express the same vibrancy. Through the intensity of His force, Śiva has the ability to do anything, and we, too, have the power of Consciousness inherent within us to create our life.

Understanding our actions is an extremely important aspect of our *sādhana*. We must learn that we are responsible for the reality we express through that power. The action of reaching is the very thing that perpetuates unhappiness; it is how we continually re-create a lack of fulfillment. We perpetually look within duality to end the pain of separation, but we can never accomplish anything on that level except reinforce the limited experience we're already having. All our reaching, grasping, and trying to change life prevent us from penetrating through duality and dissolving the veils that are causing the real pain.

KARMA IS OUR OWN CREATION

When we are stuck in duality, we inevitably create karma. The first thing to understand about karma is that there are no police watching us and there is no outside force determining our actions. It's only a question of whether we are expressing freedom or a willful intent to try to make something happen. What creates the most karma for us is the use of our will to try to compel something to change so that we might be happy. We've seen that Śiva is always expressing freedom and the joy of being alive—but due to our misunderstanding, we use that divine power of action to perpetually push and demand that life change.

what creates the most karma for us is the use of our will to try to force something to change so that we might be happy

Karma is the result of everything we do that isn't in alignment with God's will. If we function from the limitations of our tensions and patterns, everything we do creates karma. It's not necessarily that we are harming others through the exertion of our will. That is not where karma comes from. We beget karma not just in our action—although that is where it primarily gets expressed—but in our thought, in our awareness, and in how we use our God-given power of will. If God created us to express and experience joy, then all the things we do that are *not* creating and expressing that joy is karma. We have an incessant need to reach, and it extends itself through a willful energy that attempts to manipulate life. Our willfulness does, in fact, often translate into us hurting other people.

One of the actions we do regularly that creates karma for us is trying to change another person, thereby taking away their freedom to be themselves. Yet we do this all the time. It's not that we can't want something to change in a relationship, but what usually happens is that we enter a relationship out of love, but it soon degenerates into asking: What am I getting out of this? We start feeling that we can only love someone if they change, or perhaps that we can only love them if they love us exactly as we wish to be loved. We hear wedding vows that, in genuine and heartfelt words, affirm, "I love you, just the way you are." Then the honeymoon is over, and the newlyweds realize they didn't mean it!

Too often we stop loving someone because they have flaws. This is a primary way we try to change life and express our willfulness. If we don't want to create karma we have to surrender our will and consciously decide to serve. We take the force of action and project it back into God's will. Then, we are no longer trying to change life in order to feel the richness and fullness of it. We simply experience the richness and fullness of what *is*. To immerse ourselves in that resonance, we have to be quiet and feel the gratitude for the miraculous ability to be alive. This describes the unconditional joy of experiencing our own existence, vibrating in the bliss of Śiva. In this state we are complete and don't need to change anything.

SERVICE ALLOWS FREEDOM TO SHOW ITSELF

As we become more self-aware, we realize what we are doing with our freedom. We repeatedly see how the impressions of not being whole reinforce our sense of incompleteness. This is how the density of consciousness plays out in our lives. We therefore recognize that we have a problem, and that we need to stop creating karma. We need to stop asserting our will to change life and begin to channel our life force into service.

When we decide to serve, what manifests spontaneously is the opportunity to allow freedom to show itself. Freedom only exists in an unconditional state. The ego, however, has the tendency to co-opt our intention to serve others without condition. It's easy for a subtle thought-construct to creep in and suggest: "If I do this, I know they are going to change and reflect what I want." The karma of thought can be as binding as the karma of action.

we have to get very still, ask how to truly serve, and be willing to do that over and over again before we act

Our interaction with people is perfectly designed to help us understand Parāpara, the power to know ourselves. If the highest self-knowledge is "I am Śiva," everyone else must be Śiva too—right? So why would we have any need to change Śiva? Real service means giving what is wanted and needed, not what promotes our agenda. The most important time to discover how to serve someone is when you realize that you haven't been, even when you thought you had. When you are not sure how to serve, just ask, "Who am I really serving?" We use our awareness to question our motives, and the answer is often not what we want to hear.

We have to get very still, ask how to truly serve, and be willing to do that again and again before we act. Often we don't do that but just plunge ahead on our first impulse and end up serving ourselves. The third veil of duality is *I am the doer*. We believe that if we are separate, and if we are different, then we must be doing something. As we consider this veil in relation to service and karma, the hardest thing for us to grasp is the necessity of not acting. We have the power of action and our tendency is to express it before we're really clear whether an act will be of service. If you repeat the mantra, "May all my actions serve You," and let it penetrate deeply inside, you will have a twofold experience. First, everything you do that *isn't* in that resonance will show itself. Then, you can start to feel into the resonance and let it inform you about how to truly allow your actions to serve.

We have such fear that if we don't act, nothing will happen. So what? So nothing happens! Only we think something has to happen. If you are not sure, don't act. I follow my own advice: If I am not sure that what I hear within myself is God giving me a directive, I let go and surrender any need to act. Then, if the same message comes around again I listen a little more, until it is crystal clear. When we *are* sure, then we act with all the joy and force we can muster. Otherwise, we can be willful by *not* doing God's will when we clearly heard it. Whenever it's time to make a decision, it's important to really ask and not come to a verdict too soon.

IT IS GRACE THAT FREES US

In many scriptures it's said that only Śiva's grace frees us. If that is true, where does our will fit into the picture? When we recognize that Śiva is trying to free us, we use our own will to respond by doing the work of getting big enough for His grace to fully function in us. We open our hearts and establish an internal flow, creating enough space for the *kuṇḍalinī* energy to move through our psychic system. That vital force opens the chakras and begins to eat away at the denser obstruction of the *granthi*, but this is a process that takes time and surrender. We initially think that *we* are trying to free ourselves through our *sādhana*, when the highest understanding is that Śiva is doing it.

Kuṇḍalinī is the power of grace, and as her energy starts to move and penetrate through the density within us, some light begins to show itself. We realize that there is more to life than we previously experienced and we therefore use our awareness to discern what will support our growth, and what will not. Spiritual freedom is unlike anything else—Śiva is within us, in a dimension beyond our individuality. Śiva's intention is to free Himself, and we respond by opening unconditionally, allowing Him to do just that. Any resistance we express is the denial of that freedom and the assertion of the ego's willfulness.

Sometimes we do come up short, falling prey to our own will. That's why we have to start again every day, trying to align ourselves with the higher energy of *parā kuṇḍalinī*, Śiva's will. She exists everywhere, even within the depths of our resistance. Our work is to get out of her way when she decides to go home, to merge back to her source. It is Parā who penetrates back through Śiva's powers, because she *is* those powers. She functions within us as *prāṇa kuṇḍalinī* (the energy of the body) and *cit kuṇḍalinī*

when we recognize that shiva is trying to free us, we use our own will to respond by doing the work of getting big enough for his grace to fully function in us (the energy of our mind and emotions), but it is *parā kuṇḍalinī*, the energy of our spiritual self, that is awakening and rising up through the *suṣumṇa*. As more light shines in us, we also have the sense that this arousal is informing our body, mind, and emotions. Without denying their existence, we begin to see these energies for what they are—the functioning of lower levels of consciousness. We understand that we have been living from this limited awareness and ask to be changed.

THE EGO CO-OPTS POWER

The ego, however, always gets seduced by the power of awakening. It thinks: "*I* am awakening. Look at all *my* power." We can be easily beguiled, thinking and believing we're doing something—and in a sense we are, if we're using our will to serve ourselves. Hopefully at some point, grace rings a warning bell inside us and we have the courage to realize who we're really serving. Sometimes that comes as a very subtle insight and sometimes, when you just mowed down about fifty people, you see the carnage and simply admit, "Yes, I was given all this power and I used it to serve myself." Surrender is the key to spiritual freedom because it is the only thing that saves us when we realize we have usurped God's power in order to serve ourselves.

Here's the problem: We start off as a ball of energy, tension, and karma. That's our ego, and we function from that limited identity. When we infuse more energy into ourselves, the ego just gets bigger and bigger. If we engage life in order to know, rather

than to get, then there's enough clarity and insight to allow us to see where we're heading. The more we truly want to know ourselves, the less we get seduced by the power we accrue. But most people, in any field, who create a domain around them using power will fall prey to its seduction, so the issue is whether they recognize this tendency as it arises, before it's too late. That insight only comes from the willingness to surrender completely into serving others. All too often this doesn't happen, and the individual either self-destructs, or gets away with it, letting the power further reinforce their ego.

As energy rises in us, expansion takes place, which pushes up against the density of our boundaries. We experience our resistance, and we either contract in reaction, expressing our tension and ego, or we allow the density to be dissolved. In that moment, surrender is the only option, the only way to transcend the ego's capacity to reinforce itself and obscure higher consciousness. If we grab hold of the power that is trying to free us and usurp it to serve our own ego, the goddess simply says, "I'll get you next time!" *Kuṇḍalinī* has started her ascent because Śiva has called her home. Once that happens, she never stops trying to free us.

The good news is that freedom is available in this lifetime. The bad news is that freedom is available in the *next* lifetime (which is, perhaps, also the good news). The more power we have, and the more we have used it for ourself, the more karma we have created. Without even considering what we have done to the people around us, we have created our own binding and our own karma. Karma is always the result of self-serving willful action, so be conscious of not creating it. Be conscious of allowing *kuṇḍalinī*, which has exposed your karma to you in the first place, to free you from that karma.

Moment by moment, *kuṇḍalinī* is freeing us of our identity, which includes the belief that we are doing something. We even think *we* are freeing ourselves, but we are only participating. To deeply function from this understanding, to let go of doership, requires continual surrender. It's a challenge, and most people don't get it. People who have a powerful awakening taking place often get to a moment of incredible potential for freedom and then fall into a binding pattern they can't rise above. The membrane of the veils of duality are getting stretched very thin, and with one blink of not keeping that pregnancy open, the wall springs back.

moment by moment, kundalini is freeing us of our identity, which includes the belief that we are doing something

In some ways the arousal of energy is a mechanical process. But as we feel that energy moving in us, we cannot expand our consciousness without surrendering all vestiges of self-service. The veil of being the doer is so difficult to pierce through exactly because power *does* increase. You are accomplishing, people are loving you and throwing themselves at you, so it's easy to start thinking, "Man, look at what I am doing. Look at *me!*" Whatever our field of activity—whether you're a guru or not—each one of us has the same experience. That's why the greatest danger to your spiritual growth is your growth. Surrender embodies the awareness of your state and the willingness to let go of all tension and any sense of yourself.

I am personally very grateful that I didn't establish my own spiritual center until I was about fifty years old. By then, I had witnessed enough of what happens when people get seduced by power that I had some insight into the problem. I knew that there is always the latent tendency for the ego to sustain and serve itself, and the more power it gets, the more power it has to do just that. Paradoxically, it is the highest grace that gives us the power that seduces us. This is a difficult situation, and even within spiritual people the self-reflective capacity is often not strong enough to break free of the grip of power. Self-reflection, surrender, and perhaps a kick from our teacher are the means to overcoming this temptation.

Unfortunately, when a big contraction occurs, there is a lot of projection around the teacher that gets expressed as, "I don't like the way you treat me, and what you've taught me doesn't work." I once told a student, "It takes twelve years to surrender, so be sure you are doing your practice," and she asked, "Will you be here in twelve years?" I replied, "It's not whether *I'm* going to be here in twelve years . . . " She was gone in about twelve days.

there is an internal surrender and an external surrender and they are never separate

INTERNAL AND EXTERNAL SURRENDER

There is an internal surrender and an external surrender and they are never separate. As it expands in itself, energy is creating the dynamics of our life. We can't achieve a real state of freedom by surrendering inside while expressing willfulness and trying to control everything. Our experience of doership isn't primarily when we are meditating. We find it in action, in how we use our energy in the world. Usually we're not thinking about surrender when we act. We're just doing battle with life in a dualistic context, and we get lost in the turmoil. Action devours not only our experience of unity, but even the possibility of knowing that unity exists.

We have to stop and think before we act. Ask, "Where is this action coming from? Why am I pushing so hard?" We want to uncover the reason we have such a powerful imperative to control. Seeking this knowledge leads us back to understanding that we act out of desire, to fulfill our need for something. We continually act from that need, but it's the wrong action in the sense that nothing is going to fill the hole in our heart.

surrender isn't some constraint that we feel, but a true letting go

We should be careful to not overly trust our past experience because so much of it has centered around the perpetual reaching and demanding of life to give something that it can't give us. But just because that's been our experience up until now, it doesn't mean we can't reach inside and finally stop believing that we need something outside of ourself. This is a powerful stance, but turning that ship around often proves to be difficult. That's why service is so important. It stops the ship's forward momentum and gives us the power to reverse directions—to stop focusing on our needs. Then we can focus on the needs of the people and situations around us.

We're attempting to redirect our awareness, in spite of having been need-driven all our life. That sense of incompleteness is still there, and that's why we must continue to burn up our limitations in the charnel grounds. We have to incinerate those latent and not-so-latent tendencies that are perpetually trying to lead us into action. This is how we surrender what binds us and align our will with God's will. Surrender isn't some constraint that we feel, but a true letting go.

While it may take some time to fully detach from the idea of "doing," at least we make the conscious decision to "do" by serving. We're pointing our consciousness back toward our unity with God. This is why we serve and why we repeat a mantra like, "May all my actions serve You." That may appear to be dualistic—I am repeating this mantra—but it's where we have to start. Using the mantra redirects our awareness back to our source. We're trying loosen the impressions of duality and individuality by coming in contact with a higher awareness from which to act, one that is in service to God's will.

sutra fifteen

to be free of the endless traversing across
the ocean of incarnation you must see
the face of god everywhere you look.

What is it that keeps us from seeing the face of God? The simple answer is karma, which is the effect of navigating by our will instead of His. Our willful actions are an expression of tension, which are an effect of our patterns, the repeated attempt to control life, based on our own misunderstandings. That cycle is endless. Karma is not so much the form our action takes, but the willful energy behind it. It's this energy that creates the perpetual pushing we do against life—not to mention other people—trying to change it and make it fit into our sense of what it should look, feel, and be like.

Track meets often include a four-by-four relay race. The first runner carries a baton about a quarter of the way and then hands it off to the next person, and so on until someone crosses the finish line. Our karma, is a bit like that. We start out with the baton, keep running, and guess who we hand it off to? Ourselves. And then we run some more and hand it off again . . . and there's no finish line, because karma is the repetition of itself. It is the repetition of the place of misunderstanding, of mistaken desire, and the reaching we do to change life, to fulfill that desire.

There are two things about karma. We have to free ourselves of our past karma, and we have to stop creating it. Those things are never really separate. Fortunately, not every action creates karma—otherwise we'd really be in trouble because we'd be creating more of it every second! In the context of our discussion, service is how we choose to deal with both aspects of karma. Let's say that some individual shows up from a past life, or perhaps from last year. They arise out of the field of our own consciousness because we were serving ourselves when we engaged them in a previous encounter. This doesn't mean there was a dramatic ax murder last time, just that we were self-serving. When these people show up in our life, usually what we do is play the same song, do the same dance, and again fail to serve them. We repeat the same pattern of trying to control or change them, based on our tension and need.

there are two things about karma. we have to free ourselves of our past karma, and we have to stop creating it

Not every person we come in contact with is the result of that dynamic. But we have to be very aware when some relationship appears in our life that reflects a powerfully binding karmic situation. We recognize that we are the one who has to change the dynamic, and we do that by not repeating the pattern. We simply rise above the situation by not engaging the person from the same place we engaged them before. From our new perspective, we may not have to do anything except back away from the tension within us that caused us to act in a self-serving manner.

This does not mean disengaging from the dynamics we face because we can't escape our karma. We must free ourselves from it as it comes around. Our ego creates karma and it never changes. We can only be freed *from* the ego, which is the envelope karma travels in, lifetime after lifetime. Our engagement with individuals is the overt cause of karma, but that's really the result of functioning from dualistic consciousness. That's what really keeps us on that voyage of incarnation. Karma is simply the ocean of endless *saṃsāra*, how the horizontal perpetuation of duality plays out. The solution is to turn our awareness inside, internalize the energy that would otherwise perpetuate itself, and put it into the vertical flow.

SEEING THE FACE OF GOD

It's dualistic consciousness itself that creates our transmigratory existence. It's the perpetuation of "I am separate," that's the issue, and karma is only one of the effects of that underlying problem. Until we find the experience of unity, the simple experience of joy, we will keep sailing on the ocean of *saṃsāra*. That's what this sutra means by stating that "you must see the face of God everywhere." It's not just a matter of transcending karma but of not seeing duality. But guess what? You can't separate the two.

if we saw the face of god in every person we met we would just bow down

If we saw the face of God in every person we met we would just bow down. We certainly wouldn't try to change them. We would simply open—and accept, love, respect, and engage them without thinking that anything needs to be different. The experience of offering ourselves in service to the God in front of us, in the form of those people, is something we must ask for. We do that by deeply surrendering our ego, which has a limited capacity to perceive reality. Seeing God everywhere is the transcendence of duality, and while there seems to be multiplicity

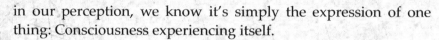

in our perception, we know it's simply the expression of one thing: Consciousness experiencing itself.

One of the ways in which we recognize the face of God in every person is to have the palpable experience of them as energy. In *śāktopāya*, living in the state of flow where all life is energy, when we engage someone, we're perceiving not a specific person but an energy field. Only we project some form around them, as we do onto everything, by defining who and what they are and are not. Life is Consciousness and energy, and in *śāktopāya* we feel the pulsation of it. Distinctions don't go away, but we recognize the unity in all of diversity. Being fully immersed in the inner experience of recognizing God in all things would be a description of *śāmbhavopāya*. We are then living in God's Presence, and God only sees Himself, no matter where He looks.

If, when we look at others—especially the people closest to us—we don't see God's face, that's okay. But we have to look again and again, and not engage with the limited face we see. Serve the people in whom you *don't* see the face of God. Try to feel what someone is trying to say or ask. Look deeper than the obvious. That takes a subtle capacity to see past our projection of other people. When we project our image onto them we're creating what they *ought* to look like or how they ought to be. We're so busy seeing them from our own perspective that we can't see the truth of the simple joy in them.

If Śiva walked around wearing a T-shirt that said *I'm God*, we'd probably recognize Him. But there's the story of Jesus knocking on everyone's door only to be told, "Go away, you're just a beggar." We have to use our consciousness to penetrate through what we think we're seeing to reveal the truth of it. It's a conscious intention to look, again and again. Students always want to know what I do and see when I'm giving *śaktipāta*. Here's the answer: I look past their tensions and suffering. I'm honestly not interested in their suffering, only in helping them live in joy. *Śaktipāta* allows a resonance of fullness to fill the space in us that, by definition, can never suffer.

LETTING GO OF SUFFERING

You will never stop crossing the ocean of incarnation if you function from suffering. You will only end that voyage when you live in joy and stillness, when there's no hard wind blowing into your sails knocking you off course. Joy is an unconditional state. We are liberated when we have freed our awareness from the notion that there is any condition that can steal that joy from us or alter it in any way. Although we do get caught in condition and allow those very things to happen, a difficult or painful experience can be a catharsis, creating a powerful change in us. But what finally ends the suffering is letting go, realizing we can find fullness in any experience if we become bigger than the contraction.

you will never stop crossing the ocean of incarnation if you function from suffering

In this regard, Rudi's death was a great gift to me. Those first thirty seconds of knowing he was gone felt like thirty years. My pain was intense. But some part of me was able to turn inside and

I was suddenly filled with the extraordinary joy of knowing *Rudi is free*. This is what he wants. Why should I be suffering about him going away? It was an amazing experience and a powerful lesson. Our painful experiences do cause us to suffer, but it is only by truly finding the joy inside them that we can be free. Otherwise, we give duality the right to keep us running around the same track, continually handing the baton to ourselves, as the same type of things captivate our awareness. When we only react to what we see on the surface of life we reinforce our previous experience.

the highest service we can give to the people around us is to not require that they fulfill our needs

Once we look somewhere new and discover a deeper level of awareness in ourselves, we see it everywhere, even in the midst of turmoil. But we have to consciously look beneath the surface, and then serve and love people unconditionally. This is how we come to see the face of God in everyone. If our life is a celebration of freedom and the expression of joy, what's going to bind us? We get back to God by first discovering the bliss, joy, and power of God's own Consciousness. That's what everything is created out of, and it's God's purpose that each of us experience His state. All manifestation and every engagement with our life is for that fundmental purpose.

God has chosen to manifest life in a way that looks quite complicated to us, so finding simplicity requires discipline, the unwavering focusing of our awareness. Specifically, we have to be willing to engage people without projecting onto them what we think they ought to be or how they should act. The highest service we can give to the people around us is to not require that they fulfill our needs. This means we have to focus on interacting with others from the place in us that does not have any need. It may be that they would, in fact, benefit from changing; that's their business. Our need to change them is what binds us.

Śiva Himself decides to free us, but like fruit, He only plucks us when we're ripe. The *upāyas* remind us that we must first do the work of freeing ourselves of the binding grip of our ego. If we're perpetually caught there, looking for suffering, how are we going to discover joy? We have to let go deep enough and penetrate through duality long enough to be free of this ocean of *saṃsāra*. We have to look to see God in everything. We confer grace on God by being open enough to receive Him. His gift to us is that we have that capacity. It's God Himself who gave us the right to have a full spiritual life, and we realize that fullness through surrender and gratitude.

When we use a mantra to ask, "God, free me from myself," it may sound dualistic, but we are really just focusing our consciousness back onto itself. In that space, what appears to be two merges back into one and the experience of unity unfolds. We shift from looking for God "out there" to experiencing Him as us, looking out. Passing through the thinnest veil of duality, we dissolve the misunderstanding that leads us to *try* to feel that God is living as us.

once you hear god speak your name and feel him breathing you, you can truly let go

God doesn't need to work to feel Himself living as Himself. He's simply doing it, and is happy about it. That's such a powerful, yet subtle perspective to gain. God replies to our mantra with,

"I'll get around to you, because you're already free" —but it's God Himself who knows that. Śiva is always living as us. Once you hear God speak your name and feel Him breathing you, you can truly let go. In that experience of stillness, the divine in us simply radiates out.

sutra sixteen
we worship god so that we may know
supreme consciousness as it knows itself.

The intention of knowing our true Self is an act of worship. If we are Śiva, and we want to know it, what greater way but to worship that? And perhaps failing to worship is an act of thievery. We're stealing God's power by appropriating it as our own, insisting that our energy is separate from its source. We're bowing down to ourselves, to who we think we are.

Inevitably, as we attempt to find God within us, the first thing we see is our ego, our separate self. We can get very dramatic about this fact, or we can simply acknowledge it and move on. Once we recognize our state, we start looking for what's *not* our ego. Then, every time we see the ego popping up, we let it go. True worship is surrender, the offering of ourself and the letting go of our small self in order to know who we really are.

The highest expression of *vimarśa*, our self-reflective capacity, is knowing that we are Śiva. That is the highest grace. We're not only conscious, but we *know* we're conscious, which is another way of saying that we know ourselves. When we know we're Śiva, there's no feeling of worshipping something outside of us. Worshipping anything external only perpetuates a dualistic experience. But where is the boundary between inside and outside? When we sit with a statue of a saint, are we worshipping a hunk of metal? If you sit there for a while, that statue starts to breathe, and if you remain there longer, there's no statue and there's no you. There's only Presence.

In truth, there is nothing outside our field of consciousness. It's only when we identify with our body that we set a boundary to who we are. The Śiva Sutras declare, "The body is the oblation." We offer that false identification into the fire of our own consciousness, thereby discovering that we are more than that form. As we throw the substance, which we think is "myself," into the fire, we ladle the ghee, repeat a mantra, and exclaim, "*Svāhā!*" It's a conscious act of offering. So few of us are able to truly understand that we are not our bodies.

Of course, our sense of self is not only tied to the body, but to the mind as well. So we must burn all aspects of separate identity. The Bhagavad Gītā says,

the oblation we offer is our experience of separateness. we use the fire of service to purge ourselves of the misunderstanding normally associated with embodied consciousness

> *I am the ritual action. I am the sacrifice. I am the offering. I am the mantra. I am the fire. I am the oblation. Those who sacrifice to Me with limited desires minimize the result of their sacrifice. Therefore you should dedicate all desire and action to Me. One should seek refuge in the highest reality because when one has realized God as the basis of all, the creator of everything, the highest knower, abiding in His own nature and self-reflective consciousness, such a person cannot be bound by activity.*

The oblation we offer is our experience of separateness. Our life has been divinely given to us as a means for achieving freedom.

Even our body has sprung forth from the sacred character of the Absolute as a vessel for holding pure Consciousness; it is the temple of God, consecrated by His own Self. When we recognize that the body is the universal body, belonging not to matter but divine light, we use our awareness to worship our creator. We use the fire of seva to purge ourselves of the misunderstanding normally associated with embodied consciousness. If we're aware of the source of the physical, we avoid being trapped in the prison of false identification with the body, mind, and emotions.

God never has the experience of separateness. Only we do—but wait a minute, we *are* God. What a conundrum! The significant difference is that *we're* aware of both separation and unity. We think: I'm having this experience, and God's having that experience. From God's point of view, He is only having the experience of Himself, whatever is happening. "I am the fire. I am the body. I am the oblation. I am the mantra . . . ." How beautiful.

THE POWER OF THE WISH TO GROW

Rudi gave us what I consider to be the highest offering: the wish to grow, the wish to know God. That starts as a mantra, but it becomes a consciousness that penetrates inside us and then is expressed outwardly as we engage our life. If we have made the oblation with reverence and faith, then we become aware of any moment when some part of us tries to sidestep our intention. When we ask, "Free me from myself," our own wish exposes to us how often we don't really mean that. We then use Śiva's power of will in us, to direct our consciousness toward service and freedom. This is the power of worship.

Whatever offering you choose to make, do it from the place of joy in yourself. What we're really sacrificing is our attachment to suffering, to the anger that arises when our needs are not met, and to the underlying tensions and patterns that keep us in pain. Ultimately, we're offering our will into God's will for the purpose of knowing that God dwells within us, as our Self. Abhinavagupta magnificently summed it up with these words: "Oblation is effortlessly offered in the fire of Śiva's intensely flaming Consciousness by fully sacrificing all of the great seed of internally and externally created duality."

Making a commitment to spiritual growth is just the first step. The real issue is whether we live up to those commitments. Our actions of offering must crystallize our intention. This is why we repeat a mantra. It's why we meditate regularly. If we truly surrender ourselves, nothing remains of unenlightened individuality. Our experience is now freed from separateness, permeated by unconditional bliss. What is it that you wouldn't offer in order to live in that state of freedom?

SUTRA SEVENTEEN

surrendering everything to god is made
possible when one attains identity with him
through meditation and selfless service.

Surrender is the doorway to God. It is our how we let go of our previous experience, and even our understanding, as we seek to approach Him. We may not initially know what surrender means, yet paradoxically, we have to surrender enough to really find out. Otherwise, any advice from a teacher or a book doesn't really resonate with our own experience. It's like trying to understand "sweet" when you've never tasted sugar. You might think, "Looks like salt to me."

A main focus of our discussion has been about serving divine will by understanding Śiva's powers and discovering that they are not separate or different from our own. When, through surrender, we have let go of our separate identity long enough, our experience of those powers is truly transformed. The purpose of our *sādhana*, of meditation, is to suspend our disbelief and lack of experience—to ask to find a deeper reality and then reach into it again and again until we have our awareness established in a new resonance. Rudi's mantra, "I wish to grow," is the drill he used to penetrate through his own pain, suffering, and misunderstanding. He did this even before he knew exactly what it was he was trying to make contact with, in the sense of having a palpable taste of it.

Not knowing is really part of the grace, because if we start with our projection of what or where we think higher awareness is, we'll probably end up drilling in the wrong direction. What we don't understand as we begin our *sādhana* is that it is Consciousness itself, arising within us, that creates the feeling that there's *something* we wish to contact. This is what brings us to a moment in which we find a practice and commit to looking for God. We now have taken our power of will and focused it.

Spiritual practices are called disciplines, because they require strength, character, and integrity. The power of our will is the strength of our dedication, commitment, and willingness to look and look and keep looking, even when we haven't yet found it—when realization is just an experience that someone else has described.

THE POWER OF MEDITATION

Meditation is turning our awareness inside to discover the consciousness of unity. In so doing, we're surrendering dualistic awareness. Looking for that inner experience of stillness and oneness *is* the act of surrendering. We're willing to let go of the experience we've had to date—that there's me and there's life—because we realize it hasn't been all that satisfying. We may not think in terms of surrender at that moment; we're just aware that we're refocusing our attention. But gaining some understanding of what we're doing is important. That's why, when people come to my practice, we give them instruction in meditation and a "wish to grow" exercise, and, from the very beginning, we talk about surrender. Students have different perspectives on what surrender might mean, so we have to discuss how it plays out in a range of dimensions. We may start with, "I surrender this thing or that idea," and move on to a deeper level of, "I surrender my tensions," and finally, "I surrender my identity." These are all part of the matrix of surrender.

We have to let go, even though we don't exactly know *how* to surrender. We just keep letting go. When Rudi said, "The only thing you have to surrender is your tensions," guess what? He wasn't talking about surrendering your tension about being cut off in traffic or the fact that the grocery store line was too long. Although all tension binds us, the most powerful tension is that of separation. As we progress in our practice and are less confused, we understand that we're trying to surrender the painful experience of duality itself. That's what takes real discipline.

although all tension binds us, the most powerful tension is that of separation

I am always amazed when people tell me that their practice hasn't advanced or that they haven't gotten past a particular issue. These are usually the same people who don't do their inner work and don't sit down to meditate every day. They somehow let life get in the way of what they said was really important to them. It takes some time to tune our awareness out of our perception of our own identity and discover God's identity inside us. We function from, react to, and extend from the impressions that are within us, based on our past experiences. So we have to meditate and repeat mantras to create a different impression. Unfortunately, what we normally repeat, moment by moment, is what Swami Chetanananda called the mantra of stupidity: "What's gonna happen to me?" That's why we need techniques to turn our awareness away from our constant preoccupation with ourselves. Using meditation and mantra, we create a new resonance that we can penetrate into, explore, and then extend from as we engage our day.

The mantras provided with this book will tune you in to a feeling that's diametrically opposite "What's gonna happen to me?" Repeating "May my will be Your will" brings us into contact with a profound openness and allows us to offer ourselves into that depth. Then, as we contact *dvādaśānta*, we create a flow with a higher force as our surrender rises and Parā's will descends back into us. This powerful practice changes our resonance and aligns us with God's will. *Śaktipāta* is another key transformative agent that works in much the same way. It starts to tune our resonance as it awakens the energy of *kuṇḍalinī*, which then rises up and informs every level of our awareness.

MEDITATION IS NOT ONLY ON THE CUSHION

All our practices are designed to turn us inside, because without doing them, most of us can't find God. We can't see Him with a depth that transforms us enough to make us realize that we are never separate from Him. Immersed in the world, we just don't see unity in all that multiplicity. This is normal, but it's why we meditate and have a spiritual practice. It's why we focus on opening our heart and establishing a vertical flow of energy inside—so that as we engage our day we are connecting from a deeper, quieter place. When we're centered inside and encounter some tension, either in ourselves or in what we perceive to be outside of us, we can digest that energy. We can convert any contraction into openness and flow.

When we focus on that internal flow, we move out of the dualistic experience that "life is all these objects out there" and begin to feel everything as part of a dynamic interchange, as energy. We surrender our perception of form as something distinct and separate from us. This is the power of Rudi's practice, which I often summarize as, "Open your heart, feel the flow, and surrender everything." None of these elements are ever separate from each other. It may be during seated meditation that we first find surrender, openness, and joy, but then we must actively remain in contact with that state by keeping our awareness internalized as we engage with what appears to be outside us.

Rudi, too, emphasized the essential Tantric teaching that meditation is not restricted to the time spent sitting on a cushion. As we feel that impression of joy inside and learn to integrate it in the flow of life, both experiences reinforce each other and become unified. This is how we break down the sense of internal and external. We've all had the experience of sitting in meditation, getting very quiet, feeling our heart open, and contacting the part of us that really wants to surrender. But we've also had the experience of losing contact with that inner awareness during the day. Some tension develops, we react, and immediately forget to even take a breath—let alone feel the flow and dissolve the density we feel. Most of our time is spent with our eyes open, engaging life, so that's where we must seek to experience unity. We have to penetrate through the tension we experience, through the patterns of how we interact with ourselves and others. This is the way we discover that we can find God everywhere and that no condition can limit our knowledge of Him.

REDIRECTING OUR AWARENESS

We are making a choice. God gave us the power of His free will and we are using it to choose a spiritual life. Not knowing what the sugar of liberation tastes like, we commit anyway, trying to understand the truth from within ourselves. Whether our eyes are open or closed is not relevant—only that we practice regularly and keep reaching into a deeper consciousness to make contact with a profound place of true surrender. Others have walked this path before, giving us the inspiration to pursue a practice that seems to lead us into the unknown. The eleventh-century sage Kṣemarāja wrote this beautiful description of what we're attempting to do: "Although the adept's attention may be outwardly directed, he enjoys contemplative absorption through introverted focus. Initially he turns inward from the outside world, and then from within himself exits into the outer world under the influence of the absorption."

Kṣemarāja is elucidating the process of tuning our awareness into God and beyond our limited perception of ourselves, of actualizing our conscious intention to experience something

we are making a choice. god gave us his own free will and we are using it to choose a spiritual life other than duality. Initially, we may only be concerned with shifting our awareness out of some pain, frustration, regret, or the self-rejection we feel. But as we move beyond all that, we find much more than the lack of pain. We discover a new dimension, a place of fullness and simplicity where none of that turmoil exists.

Once we've tasted even one morsel of sugar, we've created a new *vāsanā*, a new impression. We know what sweetness is, and we remember how wonderful it is. Similarly, as we tune our awareness out of the mundane, day-to-day impressions that determine our experience, we contact that deeper consciousness, and this becomes the resonance that unfolds out of us. Then we can engage every dynamic with new eyes. We no longer see life as something that's bludgeoning us, but as the means to finding freedom. What an amazing shift in perspective: to have no fear of life or any need to change it.

It's not only our meditation that turns us inside. Service also helps us create a new impression in our awareness. As soon as we get past our resistance and stop moaning, "I don't want to do it, you can't make me," our experience immediately changes. If, instead of allowing that resistance to rule us, we say "How can I serve you?" we've set up a very different resonance. At the end of a war, the losers don't just surrender. They sign a treaty of *unconditional* surrender.

Let's do the same in the battle with our own life. Let's stop fighting, and offer ourselves without condition: "*Thy* will be done." You can't say it and not mean it. Just repeating that mantra does two things. First, it starts to open us. Second, if we're lucky, it also starts to close us—so that we can recognize what part of us is resisting and surrender it.

In Mark Dyczkowski's book *The Stanzas on Vibration* there's a beautiful quote from the Spandakārikās. It says, "How can one, astonished by beholding his own nature as that which sustains the existence of everything, be subject to the painful round of transmigration?" We've discussed the need to free ourselves from the ocean of incarnation and how we're trapped in that cycle by all of our tensions, attachments, and misunderstandings. This is exactly what we're tuning our awareness out of. We stop fighting with the effects of sailing on that ocean—not with any sense of rejection, but with the discovery that joy exists in the same moment as our pain. We find that our individual identity, caught in the web of thought, suffering, and karma, living in the world dictated by time and space, does not exist at all! It's really a matter of pointing our inner compass toward joy long enough to create a permanent impression and then unconditionally serving as we encounter the dynamics of our life. This is what frees us from the ignorance caused by self-serving identity.

Kṣemarāja has another beautiful quote, about the power of external gaze, internal focus in the experience of unity: "With one's aim inside while gazing outside, eyes neither open or closed, this is *Bhairava Mudrā*, the most kept secret of the Tantras. By penetrating into *Bhairava Mudrā* the yogi observes the vast totality of beings rising from and dissolving into the sky of consciousness." This *mudrā* is not formed by the fingers, but refers to the immersion in what Nityananda called "the heart-space"—the infinite awareness of the chakras in the heart, the center of the head, the crown, and *dvādaśānta*. Established there, we engage life for the very purpose of learning that there is no difference between having our eyes open or closed. What we see and experience inside us, as the vertical exchange with life, is not different than what we see and experience outside of us, as the dynamic, horizontal exchange with life. In fact, Kṣemarāja is telling us that there is no inside or outside, because as soon as we perceive that, we have duality.

"May I know You as my Self" is a deceptively simple statement. It takes enormous dedication to direct our life force toward that wish, to actualize the discovery of our highest Self. How often and how deeply we open our heart and ask to surrender to God is what determines how quickly we experience that we are not separate from Him. Even the statement, "There's me and I'm part of God," is still an expression of duality. The experience we seek is that there's no "me" left to say, "I'm part of God." There's only God and His experience. We're surrendering *everything* that keeps us from Śiva, including our separate identity. All the *sādhana* we do up until that point of ultimate surrender is just practice. Janis Joplin sang it perfectly: "Freedom's just another word for nothing left to lose." That's exactly right.

we're surrendering everything that keeps us from shiva, including our separate identity

sutra eighteen

surrendering all activities to shiva, the sadhaka
is freed from the veil of misunderstanding that
he is the doer.

I am the doer. I am not the doer. I am the doer. I am not the doer. I am the doer. I am not the doer . . . . When your hand is plucking these flower petals, is the hand doing? The discussion of doership is really about what level of consciousness is functioning—and, more importantly, what level of consciousness we are aware of as we're functioning. "I am the doer" is the most confusing of the three veils of duality, even though it's simply a reflection of the others, primarily "I am separate." If there is only God, only Consciousness and its expression of itself, then of course there's no such thing as a separate entity doing something. Yet we live in and experience the beauty and confusion of diversity.

We've seen that supreme Consciousness creates the entire universe. Parāmashiva—complete and autonomous in Himself, knowing Himself—manifests all diversity out of the expression of His own joy and bliss. Since humans are created as individuated expressions of that same Consciousness, our hand *is* the hand of God. But then the question arises: If all our actions are the actions of God, does that mean God is evil because *He* does bad things to people? The answer lies in the fact that we have been given free will to use God's powers as our own. Śiva gave us life and the power to act. We have this capacity and energy, we have the power of intention, and now the key issue is what we choose to do with those gifts.

Now, the nature of our inquiry changes: How do we use the freedom and power to act, this doership we have been given? What effect do we have on others? Do we use our life force to discover the knowledge of our Self, or do we allow ourselves to unconsciously slip further away from that experience? We have to know if we are serving God's expression of freedom, or if we are serving ourselves—which only perpetuates our identity and creates karma. If we simply could, right in this moment, truly offer ourselves into serving God's will, then all of our actions would be the expression of that higher power. So what's important for us to explore is not, "Am I or am I not doing something?" because we *are* doing. We're plucking flower petals. What we do need to understand is what we're doing and why we're doing it.

WE ARE GOD'S AGENTS

If you choose to look, you will discover that the source of your power to act is not your own. It's been offered to you so that you can celebrate your life. This sutra is not telling us to stop all activity and be passive. It's saying to surrender all activities to Śiva, the source of all power. In the Bhagavad Gītā, Kṛṣṇa says to Arjuna, "Surrender all action to Me with the mind resting on the highest Self. Freed from desire and the sense of mine, abandon that you are the doer." We can't just sit around *not* doing anything for fear of being the doer. Then we'd definitely be ignoring what

God wants for us in the first place—to express fullness. So we do act, but any action we perform should be in alignment with that higher purpose.

We are God's agents. The problem is that we forget this and usurp the capacity to do and act. We fail to remember that the purpose of all action is to know our Self and experience the source of our power. Too often we use action to take control away from Śiva. He has created this life, shown us its beauty as the expression of His power, and it's complete as it is. We take that creative force and try to rein it in, declaring, "Sorry God, you got it wrong. I don't think it's perfect." We grab a hammer and start remodeling to implement our vision of what perfection looks like, thereby seizing God's agency. In addition, we attach to whatever we think our doing is going to create. This is how we become the willful doer. And what do we really create with our handiwork? Karma.

We have to stop being attached to the idea that life needs to change in order for us to experience its perfection. That takes the courage of surrender, the courage of not acting, and the courage to trust that the power that created and sustains the universe can probably handle our own life. It is only when we surrender our distrust of God that we can truly let go of the need to act. To do that, we must stop functioning from our tensions and find the capacity to rest in stillness. If we focus on surrendering doership, if we repeat the mantra, "May all my actions serve You," life goes on without us having to micromanage it.

we have to stop being attached to the idea that life needs to change in order for us to experience our own perfection

Doing mundane daily activity is not the arena that should concern us. We don't need to worry about whether it's us or God accomplishing the household chores. It's only when we have to make a decision or take some action that could have a significant effect on the direction of our or someone else's life that we must know why we're acting. We have to establish ourslevs in stillness and really ask, "Am I doing this to serve? Am I doing this to understand myself in the deepest way?" If we stop and ask, "Who am I serving?" about 90 percent of the things that we normally would blast off and do simply drop away. We see that we're *doing* because we want to control life. We feel we need something other than what God is giving us.

When we don't act, we can redirect that energy inside. This allows us to focus on finding the place in us that doesn't need do anything. This is the power of knowing ourselves. God has already given us everything. That does not mean we are all millionaires, but that we have something infinitely more valuable. We have our heart, our consciousness, and we have the simple effulgence that is always present, always with us. When we find joy inside, we trust God enough to surrender the need to control life.

MERGING INNER AND OUTER

We always have the choice to either enjoy life's wonders, or to let ourselves get caught in a perspective so limited that we only contract and create patterns of activity that continually bind us in darkness. Once we head down that second path, it goes on and on. There's only one action we have to surrender: the impulse to get something outside of ourself, driven by a resonance of lack. "I'm going to do this so that I get that," is the essence of how we perpetuate dualistic awareness and the misunderstanding that we are doing.

The flip side of that coin is selfless service—the willingness to do, without thought of price, without any need for response. Seva arises out of the simplicity of the capacity to do, and our activity is completely surrendered to God. It's the power of knowledge in us that enables us to serve. We know: *I am all things. I am perfect in my Self.* You may at first only have this realization during meditation, but once you know yourself as God, and know God as you, when you open your eyes you begin to perceive from that higher consciousness.

seva arises out of the simplicity of the capacity to do, and all of our activity is surrendered to god

In Rudi's language, life itself is always the test of whether we live that insight or not, of whether we can extend what we experience during meditation out into action. What we discover by making contact with stillness, simplicity, and joy is real—but our involvement with day-to-day life tends to take predominance over our inner awareness. That means that our consciousness isn't yet big enough to multitask, so our *sādhana* is to expand ourselves to be like Śiva, the supreme multitasker. We must also become very aware of how and when we do lose contact with our center so that we can catch ourselves and find that awareness again. What's amazing is that we don't even have to close our eyes to do that.

Spiritual growth progresses from duality, to unity in diversity, to unity itself—and that corresponds to how we penetrate back through Śiva's powers, from action, to knowledge, to will. We start with the belief that "I am doing something." That's how action is perceived in duality. Then, as we experience unity in diversity, we move into "I am part of Śiva, Who is acting through me." There's still the experience of "I" here, but we're no longer separate, and we have the knowledge, "I am doing Śiva's will."

Unity is a state of consciousness that arises when we have allowed the knowledge of our source, our own Self, to percolate up and fully devour the impressions of separateness. God exists eternally, knowing Himself to be all things, and we, too, come to know that this is our true nature. In unity we have the direct experience, "I am Śiva." I don't *need* to do anything, but if I do take action, it is the expression of my Self.

god always exists, knowing himself to be all things

The whole point of *sādhana* is to directly realize that nothing is ever separate from supreme awareness. As we offer our actions to Śiva, we begin to have the experience and understanding that the freedom we have as individuals to use the three powers of will, knowledge, and action is never separate from God's freedom. We burrow out of the density of diversity, out of the density of action, into a more refined consciousness. When we finally let go of the part of us that contracts, we can only feel gratitude and devotion. Unconditional joy is the feeling that comes from offering ourselves into Śiva's will. We've made contact with the supreme power out of which all of life was created, and know the purpose for which it was created—the expansion of bliss.

sutra nineteen

stillness is the highest form
of worship and service to god.

There are many ways to understand stillness, and every level of capacity and willingness to act from it. In this light, we can think of the *upāyas* as the means for us to experience stillness. *Āṇavopāya* is the path of our effort—whether through meditation, mantra, or service—to simply stop all the activity that we're so drawn into and caught in.

At this point in our *sādhana* we may only be looking for a way out of some pain, and there's nothing wrong with that. But as we engage our practices more deeply, the incessant demanding noise of our mind and emotions begins to drop away. We extract ourselves from the grip of the ego that is perpetually reinforcing our experience of suffering. When we take the energy of all that turmoil and pull it back inside us, we find true stillness within.

From there, our practice moves into *śāktopāya*, the path of energy, which includes the path of mind. We're now attempting to reabsorb all the energy that perpetually re-creates itself as our thought-constructs. Instead of continually trying to define life, we take that energy and pull it back inside us, into a deeper consciousness that functions beyond the grip of the mind. We experience more space inside, some objectivity with which to recognize that our opinions are just thoughts we have created.

Whether that thought is true or not isn't relevant. All thought is energy that we can consume.

We've seen that a particular thought isn't binding unless we allow it to limit us. Our thoughts are just energy projected outward, and if we internalize that energy, we can discover its source. The powerful *sādhana* of living in flow and experiencing life as energy shows us that every dynamic taking place is coming in and out of us, creating and dissolving conditions. And, in the midst of all that activity, we can rest in enough stillness to watch ourselves engage in it all with a sense that there's no need to react. We start to see and understand the energy of life from a very different perspective.

the willingness to surrender what we want creates moments of significant shift in our awareness

Sāmbhavopāya, the path of awareness, is not exactly something we practice. It's more that we're pulled into it by Śiva. This is the path of higher consciousness, of permanent stillness of mind, emotions, and will. We are simply aware, and from that awareness we experience life as it is. There's no part of us that's trying to define or change it. It is clear, luminous, and perfect. If there is a need to act, we do it from that clarity, without there being any residue of what we need to get from the action.

These levels of stillness are directly correlated with our willingness to surrender our will, and knowing when to act or not act is the first step in that direction. It's not anyone else's will we're surrendering. It's our own. The willingness to surrender what we want creates moments of significant shift in our awareness. We may be trying to force something to happen, contracting because we couldn't make it happen, or contracting because it did happen—but if in that moment we realize where all that fight is coming from and let go of it, we can change the entire energy of the dynamic. Stillness isn't an absence of noise; it is the center point of non-action, of getting past the internal force that is trying to propel us to act. We come to see that we're really fighting with ourself. We're duking it out with the part of us that wants to act, reacts with anger, and is obsessed with what should or should not have happened. Surrendering that fight is what brings us into stillness and allows us to live from that state.

There are two levels of work here. There's always an interplay between stillness and the capacity to surrender. One reinforces the other, and that's why we use the term "dynamic stillness." This is the classic chicken and egg discussion: Which one leads to which? First, by centering ourselves in stillness, we simply see that we don't have to do anything. By not acting, what is exposed is the fact that the only thing we have to change is the resonance in us from which we engage life. Then, although we may still want something or feel the need for life to be different, we can consciously surrender the need itself.

While acknowledging that there are different dimensions operating simultaneously within us, *sādhana* enables us to function from the highest. When we're quiet, when we get still enough in our heart, we recognize how much our needs bind us, and we can let go of them. That is surrender. We're not denying our needs or labeling them "bad." We just understand that the things we think we need most are the very things that bind us. We

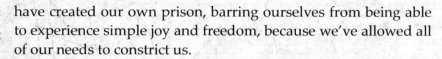

have created our own prison, barring ourselves from being able to experience simple joy and freedom, because we've allowed all of our needs to constrict us.

It isn't only the surrendering of action that creates stillness but the surrendering of our will, the force behind all action. At the same time that we let go of our willful need to act, we must also transform the energy that's attached to whatever we are trying to make happen. As we've seen, we do this by pulling the energy out of the dynamic and directing it inside. Instead of projecting that energy out through our will, we internalize it back into its source. This does not mean we cease to act, but that the energy of our activity is not outside of our consciousness.

SEEING PAIN IN OTHERS

It's often difficult to refrain from acting when we see people around us suffering, but no one is separate from God. Others' lives are also the expression of unity, and we have to apply the same understanding to their lives as we do to ours. What's arising for someone at a particular stage of their passage through this ocean of *saṃsāra* is due to their will, their karma, and God's will for them. Only a very big perspective allows us to see that. Bad things appear to be happening to them and they do appear to be suffering. But perhaps the most compassionate thing we can do is let their lives unfold. Trying to change the direction of somebody's life is a supreme act of *our* will. It takes incredible stillness to allow God's will to be done. We have to remember that the dynamics in every individual's life are a reflection of God's will functioning within them, their interpretation of that will, and the effects of their own actions. Life does not happen *to* anyone. It only happens from within them—and that means it only happens from within God.

As a teacher, people regularly come to me in pain, and my job is not necessarily to pat them on the head. Quite the contrary. When they're burning up, I might need to throw some gasoline on the fire, if that's the way for them to see how they are binding themselves. Helping others find their freedom is the greatest service I can offer. I take my stewardship seriously, but students come to me day after day saying, "I want my freedom," and their resolve lasts about two seconds. I can only serve and give people what they've asked me to give them. Too often, I watch them heading for cliffs, exercising their willfulness, and doing the very things they say they don't want to do.

life does not happen to anyone. it only happens from within them—and that means it only happens from within god

Being able to say "Thy will be done," while witnessing the suffering in the world is a tall order. So what can we do? Let's look at the people right in front of us and ask God how we can serve them and perhaps help free them from some suffering. These individuals are part of our life, so we have some karmic responsibility to try to alleviate their pain. But we generally try to free people from the pain *we* think they're living under. We project that if they do this or behave that way, then they'll feel better. What it really means is *we'll* feel better about them—and we might—but we're forgetting that we have to understand that separtaion from God is the underlying cause of all suffering.

We each must do our own spiritual work of penetrating through the pain of separtion. That's why letting people live through their suffering is often the highest expression of compassion. If you're someone's teacher or partner and they've asked you to give some feedback, then you can offer it. Otherwise, it's an act of our own will to try to redirect what's happening in somebody else's life. As always, we have to get quiet and not respond on an emotional level. In stillness we have the clarity to know when we should act, when we should give, even if we don't know the person. Any emotional reaction we have to someone else's suffering is just *our* emotion. This doesn't negate that the person is suffering, but we have to pull out of emotionality because it functions in a limited band of consciousness. If we see the world through that lens, we only get a partial picture of what's happening. It's only when we pull back, into a deeper level of consciousness, that we can see from God's perspective.

When we witness people suffering, it's natural to want their pain to stop. But look at the service offered by hospice. The volunteer's job is to be fully present, not try to stop someone from dying, but help them to do so. It may be that moving from this life to the next is what brings a person one step closer to being free from separation. Unless we see life and death from that perspective, we're only going to see their pain and suffering, filtered through the emotion of our own loss.

had to △ what I see as a problem.

The only way to know what to do is ask. Really ask God, "What should I do? How can I serve You?" It takes the stillness of pulling ourselves out of our mind and emotions to enable us to hear the answer clearly. This is conscious detachment, actionless awareness. Let's make sure we're living our own life from stillness. Then we'll have the capacity to know when we should extend and help, and when we should simply love someone and allow them to go through their own process.

Learning to rest in stillness is not easy, because we have to surrender our sense of how life should be. But if we can do that, what's revealed is God's will. Rudi talked about it this way:

> *Those who pick apart the threads weaken the fabric of creation by applying their mind to the design, because to them God's will is not acceptable as their own. We must first surrender to the miracle of creation and then the pattern will emerge. Life is composed of an endless variety of threads of many colors. The need to reduce them to a certain type of design constricts the creative output. All the tension put into the weaving is man's limitation of God's purpose.*

If we're lucky, we will repeatedly face the opportunity to surrender and find the stillness required to understand divine will. Grace itself brings us to such moments. We can only see life from God's perspective when we're not seeing it from ours. The intention of knowing our highest Self is the supreme act of worship and the ultimate expression of our self-reflective capacity. If we know that Śiva dwells within us as our Self, there is no duality in worship because we are never bowing down to anything outside of us. Established in that awareness, we rest in stillness, because we see life as God sees it—and we know that it's perfect.

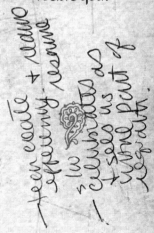

the only way to know what to do is ask. really ask god, "what should i do? how can i serve you?"

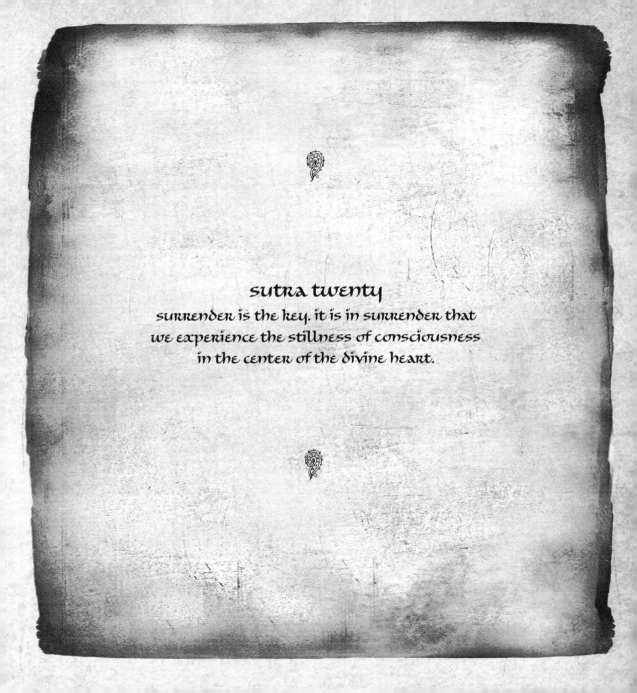

sutra twenty

surrender is the key. it is in surrender that
we experience the stillness of consciousness
in the center of the divine heart.

We must use the power of our conscious choice to find the stillness that allows for surrender, which in turn gives us a more profound experience of stillness. In this way, stillness and surrender reinforce each other, leading to an ever-deepening immersion in God's heart. We start our *sādhana* by just feeling our breath and tuning our awareness to it. As we consciously direct our attention inside and uncover more and more stillness there, everything we usually experience as external begins to be absorbed back into that stillness. Not only are we internalizing our awareness, but the stillness of breath we experience in meditation allows us to be absorbed back into the source of breath. We discover that breath arises not from the lungs, and not because of our body. Our body and breath are just the effects of the Consciousness and vital force that create and sustain us.

As we become more adept at tuning in to our breath and are absorbed back inside through that awareness, we recognize and cultivate the capacity to live in the internal breath, the subtlest pulsation within the *suṣumna*. By practicing the internal breath we discover that we are not the one who's breathing. At some point we're no longer consciously using one breathing technique or another but are just aware of the pulsation of life that is breathing us. Contacting such profound simplicity allows much of the complexity and misunderstanding of life to drop away. As we experience our source within, there's such a pregnant effulgence that it can't do anything but shift our perspective. That Presence transforms our sense of incompleteness into fullness and we let go of our thought-constructs. All this happens just by being aware of the breath.

Nityananda says to us, "Those who breathe through the nostrils are full of desire. Those who take no breath know that they are Śiva." This remarkable statement describes not only who we really are, but also reveals our misunderstanding about our identity. We think we're our bodies and minds, and believe that we breathe *because* we have a body. And, because we have a body that breathes and a mind that's held within that body—which then has a thought of separation—we begin to have the desire for something to complete us. But if we establish ourselves in the stillness of breath, we can be aware of our thoughts as they first arise, before they project us out of that stillness, into reaching for something. This is an important element in the discussion of *spanda*: becoming aware of the arising and subsiding of the pulsation of life, which creates universal breath, which creates us, while remaining centered in the source of all that manifestation.

The stillness of thought and desire is something we encounter by following the breath, but that really means following our consciousness and watching ourselves. We recognize that we have thoughts and desires, yet because there's enough stillness, we don't have to act on them. We rest in non-action, simply

nityananda says to us, "those who breathe through the nostrils are full of desire. those who take no breath know that they are shiva"

seeing the arising of the impulse to act. Even if we do act, we are not bound by our thoughts and desires, because we are abiding in a deeper level of awareness. There is never a denial of thought or desire, but we do see what dimension of consciousness they function from. And, as we've discussed, we're now aware of how the grasping for things that seem to be outside of us only reinforces the experience of duality and separation.

OUR CHOICE REVEALS THE POWER OF SURRENDER

In our practice, we start the day with meditation so that as we engage the dynamics of life, we do it from the stillness of our heart. We're *extending out*, instead of projecting our energy outside of us. This horizontal interchange then becomes a source of nourishment for us and for others, and a source of understanding instead of confusion. We have to be conscious of the different levels of energy that function within us. Then, even when we feel a driving desire, we reconize that it is a reflection of how we have limited God's highest desire for us. Having that knowledge, we can consciously transform ourselves, using the discipline of our awareness to choose which dimension of experience we are going to function from.

This is the power of choice, and it reveals the importance of surrendering that which does not serve our freedom. If we are functioning from the grip of limited understanding, we can't surrender. When we're caught in the middle of that tenacious grip we need to find a deeper awareness beneath the surface of the struggle so that we have enough space in which to let go. Otherwise, there's just no light. We can't see past the turmoil on its own level—we have to discover the stillness that underlies every level of density.

We practice the stillness of breath, thought, desire, and action, because they all lead us to the stillness of will. What is then revealed is the wonder of God's will, of this incredible freedom that is available to us. In stillness, the surrendering of our will is not an arduous task. There's no feeling of giving up what we want or of losing something, but simply the joyous offering of ourselves into a higher consciousness. This leads us to *śāmbhavopāya*, the state in which we rest in the fullness of Śiva's awareness and recognize we need not act. In fact, we know we are not the actor but just the hand of God, being used as He chooses. Stillness and surrender are not separate from each other. Stillness is the doorway into the vibrating Presence that is the Divine, and surrender is the key to the door.

stillness is the doorway into the vibrating presence that is the divine, and surrender is the key to the door

Surrender is always the key to freedom, but there are different levels and requirements of it. When we start a meditation practice, our experience is one of duality. There's us and there's everything we have to deal with in life—and we get hurt as we struggle with it all. This is normal. The work we do in this dimension is that of *āṇavopāya*, the path of effort. We begin to surrender within our experience of duality. From that perspective, we learn to surrender things, as wells as our needs and desires. Each of these levels is contained in our experience, but through surrender we understand the source of every experience.

Ultimately, we're not only letting go of all that binds us, but the very misunderstanding that we are bound. All of our *sādhana*, all of our discipline over the years, is preparing us for that possibility, giving us the capacity to surrender. It's then that we see the depth of God's grace. We see the light and are amazed by the extraordinary beauty, simplicity, and effulgence of life. In that realization, how could there be any sense of pain or loss in surrendering? We're simply offering the part of us that thinks it's separate, that cannot know its Self.

LETTING GO OF OUR RESISTANCE TO SURRENDERING

Surrender happens in every dimension of our life, but especially in service. When we're asked to do something we often have to let go of our own agenda in order to respond. We can't sit blissfully in our meditation thinking, "I am so surrendered, I feel the internal breath, all is stillness," and then open our eyes and forget what we just experienced. We are part of the diversity of life and are involved in an interchange on the level of form. Our activity must reinforce the deepest awareness in us.

If we react to a request for service with "No, that's not what *I* want to do," we have to stop, get very quiet, and recognize this resistance as the perfect opportunity to surrender. Overcoming our resistance and offering that service displays our willingness to let go of what we thought life should look like. In that moment, we may perhaps remember the mantra we repeated: "I offer myself in service, without thought of price." Whatever we have

love this
fear
(family, old,
spiritual practice

to sacrifice is meaningless compared to the extraordinary power and freedom revealed when we do surrender.

It's important to keep focusing on the reason we surrender, because when we don't, we only engage and react to life from our limited perspective. We have to keep surrendering in order to see God's will and perspective, and we're given every opportunity to do just that. We are being asked to surrender exactly those things we need to let go of, because they bind us. From this vantage point, there isn't one moment of surrender. There is *every* moment of surrender. And that applies to every dimension of our lives. At some point surrender stops appearing to be punishment. It stops feeling contracted and instead is an effusive offering into the simplicity and joy of asking, "What can I do for You today?"

surrender can be boiled down to the willingness to be changed

Surrender can be boiled down to the willingness to be changed. We all experience resistance, and that's not the issue. Encountering our resistance to change is a natural result of doing our inner work. We might also find that a lot of turmoil arises or life seems to be falling apart. All this upheaval is how grace exposes whatever lack of clarity remains within us, and we can choose to struggle with it, or let go. This is the crux of the story told in the Bhagavad Gītā. Arjuna is struggling against Lord Kṛṣṇa's command to enter battle because he doesn't want to kill his relatives. In the process of finally surrendering to a higher will, Arjuna is freed from the misunderstanding that he's doing anything. He comes to realize that everything, including life and death, happens within God.

Surrender is for our benefit, not for somebody else's. We may think we're surrendering to some person or to their needs, but true surrender is always for our own upliftment. When we experience this for ourselves and have that insight, we only look for more opportunities to surrender. By serving, we shine a light on ourselves. We see the parts of us that limit our experience, and if we're grateful to have them exposed, we're willing to sacrifice them. Our practice and discipline is to actively seek to surrender *all* that binds us—not just what we want to surrender, but everything that keeps us from Śiva.

Looking at it from that angle, surrender becomes the logical and obvious choice. How else would we answer, "Do I really want to hold on to this thing that's keeping me from Śiva?" When we're clear that liberation is the most important thing to us, we are able to offer that sacrifice. We surrender whatever it is that binds us because we know what we want in life. Not everything that we're engaged in limits us. The real binding agent is our sense of being separate and incomplete. That experience of incompleteness, the feeling of lack that leads to a driving need, is the powerful force that perpetuates the veils of duality. Feeling incomplete is perhaps a more visceral experience than that of separation.

Nothing binds us except our own consciousness. The thing that we're attached to isn't binding us. It's just a thing, an object of our awareness. Our consciousness is either bound up in thought-construct, desire, and attachment, or it's free. My own experience has been that those moments that required the deepest surrender were the most transformative moments of my life.

And if we're lucky, we have that experience regularly, because we've asked to be changed.

We must consciously look inside to discover our source and actively request, "May I know You as my Self." If we encounter some covering that doesn't allow us to see clearly, we let it go. We willingly cast off any level of consciousness we function and perceive from that has blocked our highest Self from emerging. It's never a matter of surrendering to anybody or surrendering anything; we are always surrendering our separate identity and our experience of being isolated from God. Liberation emerges from the descent of God's grace and the ascent of the seeker's devotion. These two forces converge in stillness, allowing God in and letting us out. In stillness we make contact with profound grace, in every moment of our lives.

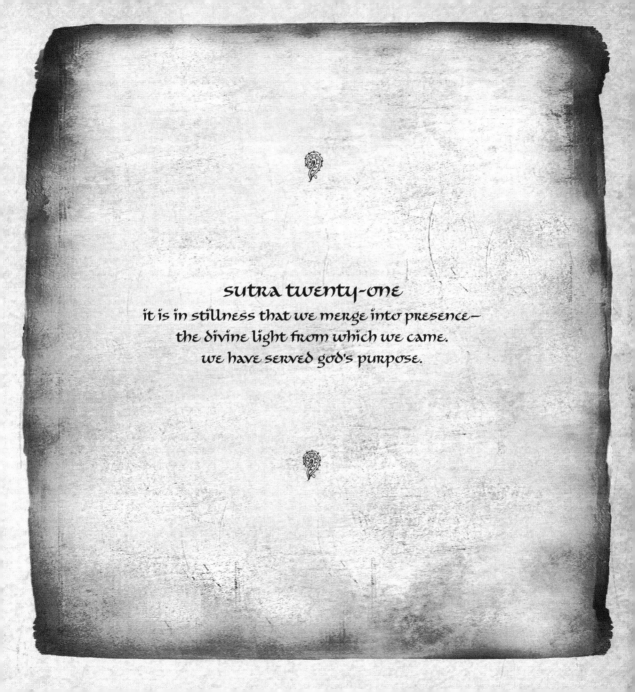

sutra twenty-one

it is in stillness that we merge into presence—
the divine light from which we came.
we have served god's purpose.

All of our practices are given to us as the means to understand our true nature, and it is our choice to use them wisely. Our life has been divinely offered to as an act of grace so that we may know ourselves, so our response to grace, in the form of our commitment to spiritual *sādhana*, is fundamental. Our *sādhana* is for the express purpose of discovering our unity with God. Whatever level of spiritual maturity we achieve is not necessarily dependent on time, although it certainly has an impact. Our experience of higher consciousness is mostly determined by the depth of our wish, the depth of our effort, and the depth of our surrender. The theme of this book has been that one of the most powerful ways we can discover our highest Self, activate it, and express it in our lives, is through seva.

I am deeply grateful for the teachings I received from my teacher, Rudi. His many gifts have continued to mature in my practice over the years—and my desire is to offer this wisdom to my own students and to those who read by books. I am perpetually amazed that Rudi's primary teaching was the extraordinary power of our wish to grow. The wish to know God gives us the capacity to experience the gift of grace, the absolute, unconditional joy of our existence. As *sādhakas*, we are choosing to direct our life force into that wish, and in doing so we are following the inner voice that is calling us home. That voice enables us to penetrate back through apparent duality, drawing us further and further into the heart of God.

All of our *sādhana*, all the surrendering of our suffering and misunderstanding, is to enable our consciousness to fold back onto itself. Making contact with our source, we find the simple stillness that is the door into God's Presence, into His state of Consciousness and bliss. It's almost impossible, and yet Śiva makes the impossible possible. Śiva's highest power is *svātantrya*: absolute, autonomous freedom. Form, no form; thought, no thought; breath, no breath—all is held within the field of unconditional freedom. The entire universe sprang into existence from the joy of expressing that freedom, and of course, our own lives are not separate from this divine purpose. God intends that each of us share the experience of His Presence and love.

god intends that each of us share his experience of the expansion of freedom

Coming in contact with Śiva's love is one of the most significant aspects of our transformation. Divine love is always present in our lives. There is never a moment in which it is not available to us. It is the flow within us that tunes our psychic mechanism so that it can resonate at the same frequency as the subtle love and bliss that expresses all of life. Then, we too have the capacity to extend that same energy out into our lives.

The expression of Śiva's Consciousness and the bliss of His energy (*śakti*) happens through His powers of will, knowledge, and action. As we follow those powers back to Consciousness itself, we become more aware within our action, self-reflective in our knowledge, and offer our will into Śiva's will. This is how we ascend, moving back through the experience of ourselves as separate individuals to the realization that we are only individuated expressions of Śiva's powers. Eventually there is no individuated identity left, because we have fully surrendered back into the source of all existence. We experience the eternal Presence that existed before we, as individuals, were ever created.

If we remember why we have this life, then everything we encounter becomes part of the process of seeking to have that highest experience. Tantric practices tell us that we are Śiva and that the most direct way to find our liberation is to simply and joyously offer ourselves to God. Let's be grateful for the grace we have in our lives, the opportunity we've been given to be free. Selflessly serving, selflessly receiving, abiding in that stillness, brings us to God's Presence. As Rumi said, "There is one thing in this world you must never forget. If you forget everything else and not this, there's nothing to worry about. But if you remember everything else and forget this, then you will have done nothing in your life."

To live in Śiva's grace, to truly access His powers in their pure form, we must penetrate through the veils of duality so that we no longer function from our individualized perspective, but from God's perspective. To do that, we must awaken the power of *parā kuṇḍalinī* within us. She is the divine power that wills life, and her energy has the ability to pierce through all the density lodged in our psychic system. I have emphasized that this internal opening

if we remember why we have this life, then everything we encounter becomes part of the process of seeking to have that highest experience

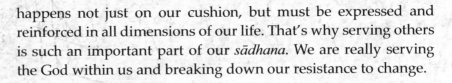

happens not just on our cushion, but must be expressed and reinforced in all dimensions of our life. That's why serving others is such an important part of our *sādhana*. We are really serving the God within us and breaking down our resistance to change.

WEARING GOD'S MALA

I've written these twenty-one sutras to bring some insight into the *sādhana* of knowing ourselves through selfless service. Nothing is real unless it's your own experience, so the mantras and meditations are designed help you integrate what we've been discussing, to let you tune in to the resonance of service that is so critical to spiritual growth. I suggest that readers embark on a 108-day journey. Put on God's *māla*. Each day, open the book and read a sutra. Reflect on what it means to you and how your experience relates to the topic. Continue to think about it during the day. In addition, choose whichever of the four mantras seems to fit best with the reflection, and do the corresponding guided meditation. Then, as you move through your day, remember the feeling of the resonance in the meditation, allowing the power of that mantra to function and work in you.

If something arises that draws you out of that awareness, be sensitive to that moment. By remaining aware of the resonance you're seeking to cultivate, you become capable of recognizing when something starts to pull you out of center and you can consciously tune back in. Specifically, see if any of the following limiting reactions arise in you, and surrender them.

I offer myself into Your service,
without thought of price—do with me as You wish

As you repeat this mantra, be aware of your response:
Is it deep fear, or joy and gratitude?
Surrender the fear, embrace the joy.

May my will be Your will

In your day, look for the times
when you express your own will.

May I know You as my Self

Become aware of when you identify
with something outside of yourself, or when
your perspective binds or contracts you.

May all my actions serve You

Pay attention to the moment
when you serve yourself.

If you do this conscientiously, you may well discover that your
resolve lasts about three seconds at a time. You recognize how
divided you really are—that there is a part of you that sincerely
makes an offering, and another part that fights to the death to
hold back. When we see how much we function from limited

awareness there's a tendency to indulge in guilt or shame, feeling, "I could have done better." Let go of all that. Simply recognize your patterns and find a deeper place from which to function.

Our self-reflective capacity of consciousness allows us to know our state and to change it. Self-reflection is the energy of *spanda*, which enables us to witness the arising of any impulse out of stillness, and to choose to not act upon it. If you're quiet, still, and centered, you will begin to discriminate between the arising of willfulness and the arising of serving God's will. You'll see it percolating up within you from a million miles away, and you can choose what to engage. This is how you begin to live God's will, consciously throwing your own will into the fire as the oblation. Spend 108 days offering yourself to God. Hopefully by the 109th day, your experience will be significantly different. You will have not only freed yourself from the incessant focus on your own needs, but you will have refocused on the highest need: that of achieving freedom.

you will not believe that it's possible to live in simplicity as long as you hold on to all the reasons why you can't live there

Our practice is not just about ending suffering. It is not about getting over ourselves or past our little struggles, but about rediscovering joy and freedom. To do that, we must stop believing our previous experiences. We think we know life—that it's difficult and full of pain—and on one level that's true. But it's only true because we have never seen beyond our own perspective, and that's why we must surrender everything we think we know, everything that has kept us locked in a limited vision of life. You will not believe that it's possible to live in simplicity as long as you hold on to all the reasons why you can't live there. Offering yourself into Śiva's joy is the decision to find a different experience. It is the commitment to eliminate all other options, because you are clear that liberation is what you want in life.

If finding your liberation is not the most important thing in your life, you will not have it. Your decision to know and serve God will be tested, and the strength of your commitment is forged in that challenge. Offering ourselves into unconditional service not easy, yet it should be a joyous undertaking. So we tether ourselves to our intention with a very short rope. We refuse to lose sight of what we know is most important. If we truly offer our lives to God, if we truly serve, we will ultimately burn through any perception that "I am separate, I am different, and I am the doer." We will have surrendered everything that kept us from Śiva. To live in and as God, to abide in and as divine Presence, is a conscious choice to serve God's purpose. Choose wisely.

PRONUNCIATION GUIDE

Trika tradition reflects the understanding that Sanskrit is a sacred, revealed language, its phonemes imbued with Śakti's power of manifestation. Sanskrit words are generally pronounced as in English, with some exceptions. Readers can use the key given here as a guide to proper pronunciation.

VOWELS

Sanskrit vowels are long or short. In English transliteration, long vowels are marked with a horizontal bar over the letter. The vowels "e" and "o" are always pronounced as long vowels.

ā	the long a, as in palm
e	as in wave
ī	the long i, as in deed
o	as in home
ū	the long u, as in pool

CONSONANTS

c	ch, as in chat
ñ	as in canyon
ṣ, ś	sh

GUIDED MEDITATIONS

To hear or download the guided meditations leading you through the internal work described in this book, go to *TrikaShala.com* and click on the Writings & Photos page. Under the Guided Meditations heading, click the link for *Wearing God's Māla* readers and enter the code WGM5 (all caps). Note that in addition to the four meditations mentioned in the book, there is an additional file entitled *The Heart Knows the Highest Knowledge.*

Paramaśiva

1. Śiva
Cit śakti

2. Śakti
Ānanda śakti

3. Sadāśiva	4. Īśvara	5. Śuddha-vidyā
Icchā śakti	*Jñāna śakti*	*Kriyā śakti*

6. Māyā

Kañcukas

7.	**Kalā**	*Omnipotence*
8.	**Vidyā**	*Omniscience*
9.	**Rāga**	*Completeness*
10.	**Kāla**	*Eternity*
11.	**Niyati**	*Omnipresence*

12. Puruṣa
Individual Subject

13. Prakṛti
Objective Experience

14.	**Buddhi**	*Intellect*
15.	**Ahaṃkāra**	*Ego*
16.	**Manas**	*Mind*

Jñanendriyas	Karmendriyas	Tanmātras	Mahābhūtas
17. *Hearing*	22. *Speaking*	27. *Sound*	32. *Ether*
18. *Touch*	23. *Grasping*	28. *Touch*	33. *Air*
19. *Seeing*	24. *Locomotion*	29. *Form*	34. *Fire*
20. *Tasting*	25. *Excretion*	30. *Taste*	35. *Water*
21. *Smelling*	26. *Procreation*	31. *Smell*	36. *Earth*

THE TATTVAS

This discussion of the *tattvas* is excerpted and adapted from Swami Khecaranatha's book, *The Heart of Recognition: The Wisdom & Practices of the Pratyabhijna Hrdayam.*

The *tattvas* help us understand how Consciousness contracts as it manifests, and how we fit in that process of contraction. Although *tattva* means "that-ness," the thirty-six *tattvas* begin by saying that supreme Consciousness and energy exist before that-ness. Before anything comes into being, there is Parāmashiva saying "*Aham,*" I am. There is no description of "I am." There is simply Being, in a state of autonomous freedom. Then, as the unfolding contraction takes place, the supreme subject creates an object; in other words, Consciousness "densifies." This is really what is happening when the *tattvas* talk about contraction. They mean that Consciousness becomes denser and denser as the entire universe unfolds.

The *tattvas* explain to us how, from within Consciousness, energy manifests the universe to become the creation of the one divine subject, but from God's perspective, none of it is separate from Him. In this process of unfolding God never loses awareness of Himself, no matter what aspect of the unfolding is being experienced. The universe is the creative expression of Consciousness, and it perpetually continues to manifest from within its center, never separate from that source. Central to the discussion of the *tattvas* is the message that although there are levels of Consciousness that continually open out, the highest level should be what we seek. The wonderful thing is that we must live through, penetrate, and devour everything that manifests from supreme Consciousness—meaning the world, duality, and our perception of everything we experience—in order to get back to the source.

The challenge is to recognize that it is impossible for our limited consciousness to understand the unlimited state. Even if we have the theoretical understanding that there is no separation, we still perceive ourselves as separate from God because our perception is inherently clouded by limited awareness. Our work is to break down all barriers to the direct realization of unity and to surrender all that we do not understand—because the *tattvas* tell us we can never understand it from our minds and egos. Just as Consciousness reveals the universe from within its center, we too reveal our universe from within our own center. This means we are responsible for our experience, and we create it from wherever we are focused in life—from our true center, or from being mired in our patterns and tensions.

All types of experience are valid and valuable on their own level, but the question is, where do we ultimately want to be established? Do we want to continue living in the limitations of diversity or move back toward unity? All of these levels of consciousness and categories of existence—all these levels of "that-ness"—are forever functioning simultaneously. And because this is true, we always have access to them, on whatever level we choose to connect to.

We must be careful to focus on the highest, because inherent in the journey is the process of forgetting. This is the fourth of the Five Acts of Śiva, the act of concealing. The first three acts of creation, maintenance, and dissolution just keep repeating themselves in an endless cycle. It is Śiva's choice to conceal, His choice to forget the very purpose of manifestation. But the *tattvas* are trying to convey to us what our experience can be— emphatically stating that we must focus on the fifth act, revealing, and that the state of autonomous freedom is the goal of *sādhana*.

It is so easy to get lost on the way back home. Anything we allow to distract us from that journey will distract us. It doesn't matter whether we get sidetracked by a stupid little nonsense thing or some big emotional drama that we think is the end of life as we have known it. If we get distracted, we get off the path and we are lost for a long time. So we need help, and that comes from grace—the revealing force that dissolves all concealment. The *tattvas* are the breadcrumbs that we sprinkle behind us, guiding us back to the experience of unity, of unlimited freedom. The *tattvas* start with the highest, so let's begin there:

TATTVA 1: SHIVA (THE POWER OF CONSCIOUSNESS)

The *tattvas* are the expression of the emission of Śiva's five powers—Consciousness, bliss, will, knowledge, and action. These are the powers of His own existence, and everything arises from them. The first *tattva* is called Śiva, and while Śiva is understood to be Pure Consciousness, it is also recognized that inherent within infinite, Pure Consciousness is an observable power. This is the source of all other powers, all other energies, and ultimately all manifestation. It is a state of dynamic stillness. This *tattva* is also called *cit śakti*, because it describes the energy or power of Consciousness.

TATTVA 2: SHAKTI (THE POWER OF BLISS)

The next *tattva* is Śakti, which is the energy that arises from Consciousness. It is the first stirring of a self-reflective quality that allows the omnipresent to know itself. And it's so wonderful to understand that the second level of awareness is *ānanda śakti*, the power of bliss, the power of joy, the power of the unconditional state of Consciousness experiencing its own existence. That joy just exploded out of Śiva. Held within His Consciousness and the power of that Consciousness is an effulgence that just can't contain itself, and its dynamic aspect begins to emerge.

Tantric tradition uses the terms *prakāśa* to denote the light of Consciousness that illuminates all of life, and *vimarśa* to describe the capacity to see the light and to recognize, "I am that light." The light is coming from "me" and creating "me" at the same time. The highest teaching is not only that we are that light, but that we each have within us the capacity to be aware of our own state of consciousness—and because we have that power, we have the ability to change our level of awareness. Śakti arises from Śiva, but it can also be the pathway back to its source, the gateway to a level beyond even the manifest value of energy or light. Śakti leads us to the rediscovery of *prakāśa*, which is beyond any form or energy.

TATTVA 3: THE POWER OF WILL

Paramaśiva is complete, simply experiencing "I am." But then an impulse arises: "What if I became something else?" From that infinitely subtle pulsation some form starts to be considered, which is described in the third *tattva*, Sadāśiva, as "I am this." Sadāśiva is also called *icchā śakti*—the power of divine will. It reveals the inherent potential of supreme will to have the intention to create, although at this point manifestation has not yet happened. Śiva stirs and thinks, "I have, through my own volition, chosen to conceive the idea of creation."

Sadāśiva means "always Śiva," or "I am this and it is always Me." At this level, there is only pure unmanifest Consciousness and the power of will giving strength to the impulse to create. This Consciousness recognizes that it has within itself the capacity to choose its experience, to choose a bigger experience than "I am." Isn't that interesting? If being "I am" is so wonderful, being "I am that" must be even greater! But remember that contained within the will to create all of manifest existence is the will to create the play of Consciousness—the play of forgetting for the joy of remembering.

The paradox is that even as forgetting takes place, every level of unfolding and every particle of creation contain within them the fullness of Consciousness. Everything in creation is already held within the field of Consciousness we call Śiva, and everything emerges because of the will inherent in that field.

As individuated expressions of divine will, we can choose to remain locked in the limitations of our own will—and God has given us the option to do just that. Or we can surrender our will and let God's will flow through us, thereby experiencing the freedom and joy of remembrance. It is only by surrendering our will that we discover that we were never the doer in the first place. Then, any idea we may have that God's will somehow has something to do with our plan for our life, evaporates. Living in surrender to God's will is a state that is not bound by any condition or any expectation of what should happen.

TATTVA 4: THE POWER OF KNOWLEDGE

In the previous *tattvas* we saw that God has the power of will, which contains the potential to create. This *tattva*, *īśvara*, called *jñāna śakti*, describes the power of knowledge. It is the knowledge of what God is going to do: expand his infinite freedom through manifestation. There is an inherent awareness of how the patterns and structures will create the universe, how energy will manifest into form. This is where awareness starts to exteriorize itself, moving one step away from the experience of "I am" to "I am all this." And yet, there is still no form. All of creation is still within Śiva's Consciousness. The interesting thing is that God is not concerned with the everyday details because His freedom is not conditioned or limited by what emits from Him. He does not need to know the details because he simply understands that it will show itself, out of its own perfection. So if it turns left or right or changes color, there's nothing that's not right. It's still part of the perfection, the expression of the infinite joy of God's own awareness.

TATTVA 5: THE POWER OF ACTION

Now that Śiva has the powers of will and knowledge, the next step is to act. *Kriyā śakti* (or *śuddha vidyā*) is the power of action, the emphatic power of expression. It is only in the doing that creation becomes reality. Śiva has the power to manifest Himself in any shape, form, energy, or operation. But, as yet, nothing has happened! All this is still percolating within the field of Consciousness. The energy for creation is revving up, like a rocket ship about to launch. This is *spanda*, or vibration; an imperceptible movement that builds on itself, from within itself, and finally just explodes into action. Out of one single essence, all multiplicity emerges, never separate from its source.

These five powers—Consciousness, bliss, will, knowledge, and action—are all functioning within infinite Consciousness, creating a self-reflective awareness of the potential for ideal form. Then it bursts forth, emitting itself as the expression of perfection. Śiva holds it and holds it and holds it, and He refines it, and then it's simply expressed as the flow of bliss manifesting as form. What we need to understand is that our spiritual work is that of penetrating back though all form, through all the diversity, past the powers of God's emission, back to the infinite Consciousness that always is. This is how we establish ourselves in that Consciousness, so that we experience it as our own Self. By so doing, we fulfill Śiva's desire to experience Himself through us.

TATTVA 6: MAYA (CONCEALING)

We now reach a critical juncture in the *tattvas*. All the potential for manifestation is waiting to burst forth, and now, Śiva adds a twist: He decides to conceal Himself in creation, just for the joy of remembering Himself again. *Māyā śakti* is the energy of veiling, of concealing. It is how Śiva hides in plain sight. We've talked about the Fivefold Acts of the Divine: creation, maintenance, and dissolution—all of which are happening simultaneously—along with concealing and revealing. The concealing is the expansion into multiplicity. The revealing is the penetrating back through that multiplicity to recognize oneness.

So while it is in the creative, imaginative, passionate power of Śiva to create multiplicity, it is in His power of *māyā*, in His power of concealing, that duality manifests. Some of the light begins to be veiled. In the first five *tattvas* we saw the beginning of a shift in emphasis from "I am" to "I am this." Now, in the descent of Consciousness, in the veiling of its own Self from itself, Consciousness starts to see "I" as distinct from itself. Although at this point in the *tattvas* the individual has not yet manifested, we can look down the road and see that because we function within *māyā*, all three veils of duality dominate our perception.

We believe that "I am separate, I am different, and I am the doer," and we experience our lives through the filter of that fundamental misunderstanding.

Keep in mind that the creation of the illusion of separation is all part of Śiva's will. Every minute particle in the universe contains the whole Consciousness, but it doesn't know it because the covering of *māyā* has come into existence. In essence, Śiva decides to limit His own capacity for perception. Why? Because the bliss of Consciousness will be even more powerful in remembering. Its value will be even greater when Śiva can look back upon Himself, through us, and discover Himself again. This is the revealing power of grace, which only happens because of the power of concealment.

TATTVAS 7 THROUGH 11:
THE LIMITATIONS OF DIVINE POWER

Not only did Śiva create the power of *māyā*, the illusion of separation, but he created further levels of concealment that limit our perception of divinity. The *kañcukas* are the limitations of God's attributes of omnipotence, omniscience, completeness, eternity, and omnipresence, and they fundamentally color how we experience our lives.

In *tattva* 7 (*kalā*), God's omnipotence is transformed into a limited capacity to do. We perceive our will as separate from God's and function from within our own resources, disconnected from divine power. Omniscience gets squeezed down into a finite ability to know in *tattva* 8 (*vidyā*)—and primarily into the inability to know the highest truth, our unity with our source. We get trapped in the restricted human perspective and can't see past it.

Tattva 9 (*rāga*) describes how God's inherent completeness is experienced in the individual as a sense of lack and the desire for something to make us whole. Because we don't have access to God's completeness and believe we are different from Him, we start looking for something other than ourselves, something outside of ourselves in order to create a sense of fullness. As we move into *tattva* 10 (*kāla*), eternity breaks apart into segments of time, resulting in the sense that life unfolds sequentially. We think something has to happen to get back to infinite unfolding, because the constant flow of Presence is not in our awareness. Another effect of *kāla* is that we have the idea that there's life and death, which results in turmoil in our mind and emotions.

The final *kañcuka*, *tattva* 11 (*niyati*), limits omnipresence as it creates space and causation. Unlimited, infinite everything-ness becomes space—and, because of time and the limiting of space, we then perceive life as causation. Then, we start doing things from a place of limited understanding and incompleteness, and the result of our self-serving action is the creation of karma.

TATTVA 12: THE INDIVIDUAL

The preceding six *tattvas*—which create fractals of the infinite through *māyā* and the limiting of God's powers—are potent forces of obscuration. They are an extraordinarily refined process of the

One becoming two. Once this is set in motion, as all of divine experience is limited and obscured, individuals and individual experience arise in *tattva* 12 (*puruṣa*). Śiva gets transformed from Himself to the individual—but at this point we're still not talking about any specific form that individuality might take, because as of yet, there is no body, mind, or ego. This is simply individuality, perceived as separate from its source.

Tattva 12 can be viewed as the beginning of the fundamental misunderstanding of our separation—but in terms of spiritual growth, it is also the entryway back into unity. Individuation marks a *bindu* point, a singularity of focus, where Śiva pushed us from oneness to duality, but Śiva's grace can also pull us back up through that same *bindu*. Although we have been discussing the *tattvas* in terms of the descent of Consciousness into more density, it's at this juncture that we have to start considering ascending and descending at the same time.

Tattva 12 is the point where you either ascend back up, or you don't. All of the *tattvas* below this are expressions of how the individual's experience gets entangled in form, and by our mind, emotions, and ego. If we can transcend those levels of density on the way back up, we have the opportunity to surrender the last barrier to living in unity—our separation from God.

Remember that Śiva concealed Himself in separation, because it's all about the joy of recognition, the joy of opening our hearts and experiencing unconditional freedom. The whole purpose of individual experience is creating the potential for billions of little

Śivas to remember that they are the one light of Consciousness, the light that illuminates life. We'll return to a discussion of why *puruṣa* is such a critical pivot point on the journey to freedom, after having presented the remaining *tattvas*.

TATTVA 13: OBJECTIVE EXPERIENCE

Almost simultaneous with the arising of the individual, is *tattva* 13, *prakṛti*, or objective experience. *Prakṛti* gives rise to materiality, meaning that matter and energy take on the structure of form, including the human body. It is at this moment that the process of Consciousness forgetting itself is complete. Our experience of having forgotten our source is the effect of *puruṣa* and *prakṛti* coming into existence after the creation of the veils of duality and the limiting of God's powers. Because those forces of concealment are already in place when individuality and materiality come into being, we are born into the belief that there is a separation between subject (us) and object (everything else).

From the highest perspective, there is only Śiva—breathing and pulsating as every individuated expression of Himself. On that level there is no separation between the individual and the objects perceived by the individual. Although Consciousness has now descended from Its highest state of infinite freedom into multiplicity, from Śiva's point of view, all that exists is held within infinite freedom. From a spiritual understanding, we are made up of all the divine powers we have discussed, carefully folded together to create the individuated expression of that whole. Individuality and the ability to perceive form are not limiting unless we choose to make them so.

It is our choice to look "up" toward our source or "down" toward obscuration. We have, in a sense, let Śiva trick us into misconstruing His will, which is simply the expression of joy and freedom, in whatever form it takes. There is no pain or suffering inherent in individuated experience, but we turn form into suffering by trying to make things different, losing the capacity to truly experience our life as perfect, exactly as it is. Perfection is not defined in form, only in consciousness, only in unconditional awareness.

TATTVAS 14 THROUGH 16: INTELLECT, EGO, & MIND

The challenge for us as individuals is the interpretation of our experience. This is complicated by the fact that individuated consciousness, having formed a body, starts to have intellect (*buddhi*), ego (*ahaṃkāra*), and mind (*manas*). Ego and mind, in particular, are what really trap us in our limited perspective.

Buddhi, *tattva* 14, is the capacity to recognize, formulate, and make decisions. It is the power of discernment, albeit a limited power of discernment. What's important to point out here, in terms of the descent of Consciousness, is that intellect arises before mind and ego. *Buddhi* is still part of higher Consciousness— before it is put within the grip of mind and ego, our own thought-constructs. Those thought-constructs are always about "me." They are always about distinction and trying to fix distinction.

Buddhi just recognizes distinction and is fine with it. This is why decisions made based on discernment are less limited than decisions we make from our mind, and far less limited than those we make from our ego.

We spend considerable time talking about the ego (*tattva* 15) because it is that part of us that can't see anything but itself, and it exists in a state of separation. *Ahaṃkāra* is the Sanskrit term for ego, and, interestingly enough, the word starts with "*Aham*," I am. The problem is that *ahaṃkāra* means "I am me." Śiva doesn't need to say "I am Me." He just says "I am." Our ego makes a projection of ourselves that is not based in reality because it believes, "I am separate from myself."

All struggle comes from the ego's determination to sustain its separate identity. We have a complete misunderstanding of who we are, and we project our lives based on that misunderstanding. Then, we work very hard to remain on that level of consciousness! We are, in fact, so attached to that misunderstanding that we feel we have to dig in and defend it, which only locks us more deeply in concealment.

This is where, at *tattva* 16, *manas*, or mind comes into play. Mind is a tool of the ego. We might even say it's a cancerous growth within ego. Thought-construct seeks to maintain the belief in separation, and this is why Abhinavagupta says that thoughts are the source of all bondage. Liberation is only possible when we can free ourselves from the incessant chatter of the mind and the grip of the ego. If we understand this, we recognize that the pathway back to higher Consciousness is the consuming of the energy and the limited understanding of mind and ego. We internalize this energy into our psychic body, creating a flow within, pulling our awareness out of the level of mind and ego, and letting the psychic body refine that density of consciousness. In this way, we transmute density into fuel for our internal growth.

TATTVAS 16 THROUGH 36: THE DENSIFICATION OF CONSCIOUSNESS

These *tattvas* represent the further contraction of Consciousness into matter. Looking at the chart, we can see that they fall into four basic categories: the powers of perception and action, and the subtle and gross elements. These *tattvas* are the world we live in. In terms of our spiritual growth, we seek to internalize the energy contained on these levels in order to transcend the misunderstanding that our interaction with material life is something outside ourselves.

Swami Khecaranatha has practiced and taught Kuṇḍalinī Sādhana since 1972. With a mastery etched from more than four decades of dedicated inner practice and selfless service, he is an authentic adept of nondual Trika Shaivism and an initiated lineage carrier in the *śaktipāta* tradition of Shri Bhagavan Nityananda and Swami Rudrananda (Rudi). Based on the profound spiritual transformation he experienced in his own life through the practice of Kuṇḍalinī Sādhana and the grace of his teachers, he offers inspirational and practical guidance that can change a reader's life as well.

Khecaranatha was born in 1951 in Illinois in circumstances comparable to those of most of his students and readers. His own life has demonstrated that it is possible to live fully in the world while developing and maintaining one's conscious connection to the divinity within. After meeting his teacher Rudi in 1971, Khecaranatha moved into the ashram in Indiana, and Rudi recognized him as a teacher within this lineage in 1972.

After Rudi took *mahāsamadhi* in 1973, Khecaranatha continued to work with Swami Chetanananda, the spiritual leader of the ashram, and lived as a member of that community as it subsequently moved to Cambridge, Massachusetts, and finally to Portland, Oregon.

Serving as the head teacher under Chetanananda, Khecaranatha was, through the years, instrumental in helping to develop the ashrams that Rudi started. While living in an ashram for thirty years he also held several "real-world" jobs, including that of CEO of a multimillion-dollar consulting business. This personal experience strengthened his conviction that there is no separation between spiritual life and life in the world.

In 2001 Khecaranatha moved to Berkeley, California, to start Sacred Space Yoga Sanctuary, a spiritual center. Sacred Space offers in-depth instruction in Kuṇḍalinī Sādhana through its TrikaShala program. In addition to teaching, Swami Khecaranatha currently serves as director of Rudramandir: A Center for Spirituality and Healing, which is operated by Sacred Space.

In July of 2002, Khecaranatha took formal vows of *saṁnyāsa* and was initiated into the Sarasvatī order by Ma Yoga Śakti, a swami based in New York. He was given the name Swami Khecaranatha, which means "Moving in the fullness of the divine Heart." A swami, or *saṁnyāsin*, is unconditionally committed to serve, love, and support other people in their spiritual growth. To fulfill that undertaking, Khecaranatha continues to teach and to serve as the spiritual leader of a community of practitioners at TrikaShala.

About TrikaShala and Rudramandir

Swami Khecaranatha is the spiritual leader of TrikaShala, the meditation program at Sacred Space Yoga Sanctuary, a nonprofit organization in Berkeley, California. TrikaShala teaches Kuṇḍalinī Sādhana through classes, retreats, immersions, and engagement with a spiritual community. Weekly classes, which include *śaktipāta* transmission, are free of charge. For more information about attending your first Kuṇḍalinī class or retreat, please call (510) 486-8700 or visit *TrikaShala.com*.

TrikaShala is located at Rudramandir: A Center for Spirituality and Healing. Its mission is to serve the community by offering a breadth of programs to aid in the exploration of each individual's full potential. The experience of celebration and expansion at Rudramandir is enhanced through the adornment of the space with sacred art in the form of sculpture, painting, and architectural elements, evoking the magnificence of Spirit. Additional information is available at *Rudramandir.com*.

34805144R00191

Made in the USA
Charleston, SC
15 October 2014